The Dilemma of Popular Sovereignty in the Middle East

Power from or to the People?

Edited by

Kingshuk Chatterjee

Priya Singh

Institute of Foreign Policy Studies (IFPS)

Centre for Pakistan and West Asian Studies (CPWAS)

Calcutta University
Kolkata

in association with

KNOWLEDGE WORLD

KW Publishers Pvt Ltd
New Delhi

The **Institute of Foreign Policy Studies** (IFPS) at the University of Calcutta is an autonomous centre devised for the study of international relations, with particular emphasis on foreign policy. Funded by the Ministry of External Affairs (MEA), Government of India, the institute purports to create a pool of foreign policy specialists capable of offering advice on matters pertaining to India's international relations. The Institute has already been earmarked for developing regional expertise with reference to the Government of India's Look East Policy, and that towards West Asia. The IFPS has also been chosen as one of the ten centres for United Nations Academic Initiative, functioning as the hub for studies on peace and conflict resolution.

The **Centre for Pakistan and West Asian Studies**, Calcutta University, was set up in 2005 under the UGC Area Studies Programme. It is the only research outfit associated with a University in eastern India with an exclusive focus on Pakistan and West Asian countries, Afghanistan, Iran and Iraq in particular, which together constitute a part of India's extended neighbourhood in the West. The Centre, since its establishment in 2005, has tried to develop a greater understanding of this extended neighbourhood by looking at the internal dynamics of the region with far greater detail than is generally accorded by other area studies outfits in the country.

ISBN 978-93-83649-11-2

Published in India by Kalpana Shukla

KNOWLEDGE WORLD

KW Publishers Pvt Ltd
4676/21, First Floor, Ansari Road, Daryaganj, New Delhi 110002
Phone: +91.11.23263498/43528107
Email: knowledgeworld@vsnl.net • www.kwpub.com

Printed and Bound in India

2011 FPBA BEST PUBLISHERS AWARD (ENGLISH)

Contents

List of Contributors

Joseph Alagha is a Professor of Cultural Studies at Haigazian University, Beirut.

Waiel Awwad is the South Asia Bureau Chief, Syrian Arab News Agency, New Delhi.

Kingshuk Chatterjee is an Associate Professor in the Department of History, Calcutta University.

Srinjoy Chowdhury is the National Affairs Editor, Times Now.

Mehmet Ozkan is a lecturer at the Department of International Relations, International University of Sarajevo, Bosnia-Herzegovina.

Mudassir Quamar is a doctoral candidate at the School of International Studies, Jawaharlal Nehru University.

Anita Sengupta is a Fellow at the Maulana Abul Kalam Azad Institute of Asian Studies.

Priya Singh is a Fellow at the Maulana Abul Kalam Azad Institute of Asian Studies.

Mary Totry is Professor of Women's and Gender Studies, Faculty of Humanities at Haifa University, Israel.

1. Introduction
Power from, or to, The People?

Kingshuk Chatterjee

In January 2011 as winds of change began to blow in the Arab world and authoritarian regimes began to appear vulnerable, observers were quick to label it as the beginning of the so-called "Arab Spring." With at least four dictators (Ben Ali of Tunisia, Mubarak of Egypt, Abdullah Saleh of Yemen and Muammar Qadhdhhafi of Libya) toppled, and an array of reforms (in Jordan, Bahrain, Saudi Arabia) introduced, the label was able to vindicate itself quite handsomely. However, with two bitter civil wars being fought (in Libya and Syria), one of them now running into its third year, and at least one movement being ruthlessly subjugated (Bahrain); observers have begun to pronounce that the Arab Spring has turned somewhat mellow.

The turmoil in the region was being labelled 'spring' because it was expected to lead to the blooming of a new political era when the people would enjoy access to political power, ending the 'winter' of authoritarianism. However, as outfits motivated by Islamist agenda (al-Nahda in Tunisia, Ikhwan al-Muslimin, i.e. the Muslim Brotherhood, and Hizb al-Nour in Egypt) made the largest gains in the elections that followed, some crucial questions began to be raised about the character of change that the region was witnessing. As (for want of a better word) Islamists began to take measures to implement their agenda, the freedoms that had been fought for and/or taken for granted appeared under threat. The conduct of the Egyptian Ikhwan in particular, allowing acts of hostility against the Christian minority and curtailing social freedoms that even the dictatorship used to allow, made Egyptians ask: What does 'power to the people' actually mean? Power for what? Does a government elected by a majority of the people enjoy the authority to do whatever it pleases to the detriment of a section of the people who may or may not have voted for the government? If such a government tramples on the rights of some people, is it either necessary or desirable to allow it do so till it can be voted out of power? Can a government that tramples on, and restricts the scope of, rights of some or all of the people even claim to have any kind of legitimacy that needs be heeded, regardless of the size of the mandate they may be said to have commanded at the time when elections were held?

These questions were significant *because* they could cut both ways. If President Morsi and the Ikhwan were in violation of the spirit of the upheaval that toppled Mubarak, how does replacing Morsi with the military yet again square up with the spirit of 2011? If ascendancy of the Islamist political forces impaired those (Muslims and non-Muslims) who do not subscribe to the agenda, then does ascendancy of the secularists also not impair those who do not share *that* agenda? Were either of these agenda more legitimate than the other? If the Morsi regime had not been able to do justice to the hopes of the people who made up the crowd at Tahrir Square, should that be a good argument to keep Bashar al-Assad in power in Damascus lest Islamists gain similar ascendancy there as well? Most importantly, in situations of civil war, (as in Libya in 2011 and more particularly Syria 2011 onwards) when both sides enjoy considerable popular support, where and how does one locate legitimacy?

Admittedly, contrary to what most observers seem to think, the turmoil of the so-called "Arab Spring" is far from over – and not simply because of the civil war being waged in Syria. None of the countries that ousted authoritarian regimes have seen the successor regimes meaningfully address any of the issues that brought about the turmoil in the first place – Morsi has already been toppled, but there is no comfort zone in Tunis, Tripoli or Sanaa either. Also, where the regime could not be changed, the agenda of change has not necessarily been defeated – viz. reforms in Amman and Riyadh have not stalled; Manama is also keen on resolution of issues rather than persisting with the brutal repression that characterised its response in 2011. It is thus necessary to understand the dynamics of an ongoing process that 2011 merely initiated; it is not time yet for a post-mortem.

At the heart of the matter, not merely in the Arab world but the Middle East as a whole, seems to be the question of the nature and incidence of sovereign authority in a state. In the modern era, states have progressively tended to broaden the social basis of power. Although the manner in, and the extent to which, the social basis of power has actually been widened has tended to differ from country to country, region to region, yet the general drift towards such broadening has not been region or culture specific. As the language of politics changed in course of the 19th and 20th centuries, regimes all across the world began to conform to the cardinal benchmark – laws formulated by the government have to visibly promote the interests and well-being of the people, rather than those of an individual, a group or a section of the people. By the middle of the 20th century, it was hard to find a regime that did not establish its legitimacy to rule by means of its claim to represent the interests of the people – regardless of how such 'interests' and 'people' were defined. Popular sovereignty was here to stay.

However, there remained major ambiguities in the concept of popular sovereignty, which derived from contested understandings of the category of 'people' and the meaning of 'sovereign'. Who are the 'people'? Does the category of 'people' stand for a particular sort of people, or does it include everyone? How does one discern 'interests of the people?' Do 'interests of the people' connote the interests of the majority, or does a particular type of interest get prioritised in the running of the state? Either way, what of those who disagree? Do they remain included in the category of the 'people', or do they get excluded from the ranks of those who remain the legitimate concerns of the state?

A second and related ambiguity revolves around the question of representation. How does the government, (which is a group of individuals) *represent* the interests of the people, (which is a much larger group of individuals)? In a state where the cardinal institutions of representative democracy (rule of law, elected legislature, elected executive accountable to the legislature, free and independent judiciary, free press, etc.) are well entrenched, elections are accepted as the best way possible to go about resolving the issue of representation. However, when such institutions are not quite well-entrenched (viz. any source of power that is not accountable, muzzled press, dependent judiciary, etc.), it is difficult to imagine elections as a definitive resolution of the matter.

Such ambiguities have resulted in a two-fold classification of regimes in terms of their approach to the issue of popular sovereignty. The minimalist approach to popular sovereignty classifies regimes as fully authoritarian only if there is no scope for representative politics at all. Any regime that allows for representative politics qualifies as 'electoral democracy,'[1] which the minimalists argue to be the essential feature of popular sovereignty, i.e. "the people have the right to determine who governs them ... and hold [the government] accountable for their actions. Democracies also impose legal limits on the government's authority by guaranteeing certain rights and freedoms to their citizens."[2] By this yardstick, among the Middle Eastern states Iran, Israel, Lebanon and Turkey would qualify as having institutionalised democracy, and thus acknowledging the principle of popular sovereignty; Tunisia and Egypt seem to have qualified as such in 2012, and Iraq could be argued to have done so as well after holding elections (albeit under American aegis). In the maximalist parlance, though, popular sovereignty involves what is construed as a 'proper' democratic order, (which Freedom House calls 'liberal democracy') a substantial array of civic and political liberties (viz. civic equality, rule of law, freedom of speech, freedom of assembly, freedom of movement, freedom of faith, etc.) are considered indispensable for popular sovereignty to attain its fullest perfection.[3] By that yardstick, none of the Middle Eastern states, Israel included, enjoys popular sovereignty.

The Arab Spring, and indeed the ongoing political turmoil in the Middle East as a whole (let us not forget the churning in Turkey, Israel and Iran on the northern, southern and eastern rims of the Arab world) would seem to be essentially a contest between the minimalist and maximalist positions on popular sovereignty: should power merely come from, and be exercised in the name of, the people? Or, should those in power be fully accountable to the people? The dilemma is considerable; and it is real. It is also unlikely to be resolved overnight – hence it warrants a closer look.

The present volume comes principally out of an international conference held in Calcutta, India by the Institute of Foreign Policy Studies and the Centre for Pakistan and West Asian Studies, University of Calcutta in March 2013. Neither the conference, nor this volume, was aimed at a definitive analysis of why what happened did happen. Both were instead at getting a sense of *what* was actually happening, and what is at issue. Accordingly, (and we would like to believe, appropriately), in the first cluster of essays, we have tried to bring together some first-hand experiences of the turmoil through voices from and of the region itself. The first essay is by an Indian journalist Srinjoy Chowdhury, who speaks of his experience of the momentous days of January-February 2011 at the Tahrir square – listening in to, and making sense of, what the people were saying as they went about dislodging one of the longest serving rulers in our times. The second essay by Mary Totry deals with the motivation and expectation of Arab women as they emerged equal stakeholders in the turbulence of 2011, and also the extent to which they ended in disappointment. The third essay is, so to say, from the other side of the debate as the prominent Syrian journalist Waiel Awwad mounts a passionate, if somewhat polemical, attack on the nature of the opposition forces participating in the Syrian civil war. Awwad warns us that any axiomatic assumption that the opposition forces constitute a progressive force for change would be completely wrong, and disastrous in its consequences.

The second cluster of essays deals with the question of (Islamic) identity and the manner in which it feeds into any debate on popular sovereignty in the region. Joseph Alagha deals with the question with respect to Lebanon, and argues Islamic ideology/identity is incidental to the discourse on sovereignty and not an intrinsic feature. He shows how the Hizbullah, which came to power in Lebanon *before* the turmoil championing sovereignty of the people, has compromised itself ideologically by supporting the Syrian regime in Damascus *against* the people. Mehmet Ozkan's essay on the experience of Islamist politics in the Republic of Turkey, on the other hand, strongly argues that the ideological character of the Islamist agenda is intrinsically attuned to the question of empowering the people. Studying the context in which the Islamist constituency has grown in Turkey (and by inference, elsewhere) in the backdrop of inequitable social and political orders, Ozkan aims to provide an insight into the character of the turmoil that is now raging in the Middle East. Anita Sengupta however raises questions about the efficacy of transposing the Turkish experience as a road-map on the Arab Middle East. Indicating the particularities of the trajectory of the evolution of the discourse on politics and the permissible role of Islam within it, Sengupta makes a strong case that this is perhaps the one model which, as it stands, cannot be foisted elsewhere.

The third cluster of essays deals with the experience of three countries where (despite the absence of any discernible turmoil) the political discourse revolves as much around the question of popular sovereignty as it did in any of the other countries where it manifested in a spectacular manner. Looking at the unabashedly authoritarian Kingdom of Saudi Arabia, Mudassir Quamar argues that serious efforts are underway to dismantle the edifice of authoritarianism. He contends that the monarchy has been sensitive towards the demands of the people in response to the Arab Spring, without compromising on the state structure and the political system. In her essay on the state of Israel, Priya Singh deals with the thorny question of citizenship in the Jewish state to argue that the propensity to very narrowly define the category of citizen and its relationship with the state is impacting the notion of sovereignty there. She indicates a sense of movement and points to serious complications/ruptures and perhaps momentous transformations in the economy, politics, citizenship, religious/secular divisions, and Jewish/Arab relationships. To the extent that state of Israel as it stands today is distinctly different from the one that was formed in 1948. Kingshuk Chatterjee's essay on Iran makes the case that unlike most other countries in the Middle East, the Islamic Republic provides much greater room for the principle of popular sovereignty. Using the popular disturbances around the disputed outcome of the 2009 Presidential elections, he argues that the demand for greater accountability of those in power has grown over time, and despite considerable resistance from the conservative elements in the body-politic, looks all set to acquire critical mass in the foreseeable future.

Notes

1. Freedom House lists four benchmarks for 'electoral democracy': "1)A competitive, multiparty political system"; (2) "Universal adult suffrage for all citizens"; (3) "Regularly contested elections conducted in conditions of ballot secrecy, reasonable ballot secrecy, and in the absence of massive voter fraud, and that yield results that are representative of the public will"; (4) and "Significant public access of major political parties to the electorate through the media and through generally open political campaigning. "See Freedom House, *Methodology*, (New York and Washington DC: Freedom House, 2008) pp. 9-10, http://www.freedomhouse.org/template.cfm?page=351&ana_page=341&y [accessed on 9th July, 2012]
2. Michael J. Sodaro, *Comparative Politics: A Global Introduction*, (New York: Mc Graw Hill, 2004). p. 31.
3. For a brief but informed discussion of the minimalist and maximalist notions, see, David F.J. Campbell, "the Basic Concept for the Democracy Ranking of the Quality of Democracy" (Vienna: Democracy Ranking, 2008), http://www.democracyranking.org/downloads/basic_concept_democracy_ranking_2008_A4.pdf, accessed on 9th July, 2012.

2. Tahrir

Srinjoy Chowdhury

In the war against tyrants, idealists and the impoverished are often unlikely allies. While Liberty, Equality, Fraternity once rubbed shoulders with the infamous 'Let them eat cake' declaration, Egypt's Arab Spring, lacking a resident Rousseau, wasn't short of Facebook-fuelled outrage. It wasn't short of television cameras either – this was the story of the day. The world was watching: would a million protesting voices prevail in this latest version of David vs Goliath? Or would the Arab World's beacon and also, one of the world's oldest civilisations, continue to be led by a venal and vindictive dictator?

My story of Tahrir Square is that of a journalist, about the medley of voices of the Revolution, about thousands of demonstrators with one objective, one goal, one ambition—the removal of Hosni Mubarak, vice-president of Egypt for six years, and then, the country's President for 30. It is a series of vignettes of the sights and sounds of Arab Spring's Ground Zero.

Protest does not come easily to people. Why does a man or woman leave the comfort of his or her house, walk away from family and friends, a job (if there is one) and spend time in a Square day after day after day, not knowing when he or she will get home, come back alive, come back victorious? How resentful does one have to be to do something like this? Designed for the world's cameras, the posters of *Tahrir* (liberation in Arabic), are a journey into the minds of people demanding change, people desperate for it. In their own, often crude way, the posters tell the story of revolution. One, as a statement on the sclerotic Egyptian state, without being clever or creative, had no parallel. Ten black-and-white photographs in two columns was all there was. One column had photographs of American Presidents—Ronald Reagan, George Bush, Bill Clinton, George W. Bush and Barack Obama. On their right was the same photograph of the same man: Mubarak. America went through five Presidents in 30 years. It endured Iran-Contra, the first war in Kuwait, a President's impeachment because of an intern, 9/11, unpopular wars in Afghanistan and more economic woes. On the other hand, Egypt had only Mubarak, leading a society nowhere near a Utopia, nowhere near providing a growing, restive population of about 80 million with what it needed. Add to that the inability of the people to express themselves fully, people aware they cannot vote their leader out even if they wanted to.

Thirty years is a long time to be President, particularly if you were not democratically elected, if you have not consulted your people. There were millions in Egypt—young adults and adults who knew about the world but hadn't seen anything beyond Mubarak as President. In those three decades, India had seven parliamentary polls and nine Prime Ministers to deal with issues as diverse as assassination and riots, the Bofors scam, the Mandal agitation, communal violence, a new economic policy, nuclear tests, war with Pakistan, the Indo-US nuclear deal, 26/11 and a series of debilitating scams. In both India and the United States, the people decided; the people marched to the polling booths and not on the streets, jettisoning leaders if they didn't like them. Which is why the agitation in New Delhi in 2011, led by social activist Anna Hazare, for all its fervour, lasted two heady weeks and gently, came to an end. In Egypt, in the midst of economic troubles, a pressure cooker called Mubarak persisted. Historians may explain one day why the explosion didn't happen earlier, whether the tinder was there and all that was necessary was the spark that the Tunisian uprising eventually provided.

Even before I got to Tahrir, at Cairo airport itself, I realised Egypt had a problem. If a foreign correspondent comes to India, would anybody even wonder why he's bringing in a television camera? It wouldn't occur to our customs people, who are more worried about gold-bars and electronic goods. At the airport, that's the first thing we were asked.

"Do you have a TV camera?"

Yes, of course. We're journalists.

"Do you have a permission to bring in a camera?"

We didn't know you need a permit to bring a TV camera in. Where can you get one?

When you ask how you get a permit, you are moved from one part of the airport to another, from one desk to another; from people who aren't at their desks to people who won't tell you anything, to people who say they don't have the authority to give you permission. When you know there is no way out you'll hand over your camera, you exchange it for a piece of paper with a stamp on it. You then look for the nearest taxi-driver who will steal you blind but will at least, get you to Tahrir Square.

This is a world journalists know. This is a world we budget for. For, we did hand over a camera. But once we got to Cairo, once we were at Tahrir, we got our work done. Simply because we took a slight risk—once we handed over a video-camera knowing we may never see it again, we were waived through quite quickly. What use is a TV journalist without a TV camera? Except, we had a second camera, and nobody asked if we had another one. And that's how we were able to work without much trouble till trouble began chasing people with cameras. There were Mubarak's goons on one side of the Square either discouraging you to use a camera, confiscating them or breaking them. So, what do you do then? You thank technology and use the camera in your mobile phone.

But the big point isn't really that, what kind of regimes would have restrictions against video-cameras? Why restrict cameras unless you're worried about what pictures would go out to the world? Why worry about what pictures will go out unless you have something to hide? And if you're so worried about hiding what's going on in your country, what kind of government are you?

As battles go, it was familiar enough—an aging tyrant, out of touch and let down by a determinedly neutral army that ruled out a bloodbath, hoping, perhaps, that the people who wanted him out would lose patience and go away. But they didn't, these thousands, till the tyrant was overthrown and the memory of the lost yesterdays were exorcised.

So, who were the thousands at Tahrir? What kind of people were they? There were men, women and even children. There were young people, elderly people. Some people were clearly well-off. Others were more working-class, more middle-class. There were a lot of women in the Square, and again, from different sections of society. Some were clearly conservative, in hijabs or at least, headscarves; others were wearing jeans. Many were middle-aged, many had brought their children along. And they weren't afraid to speak. It was an obstacle race—the road to Tahrir from other parts of Cairo, said one woman, the authorities doing their best to stop people from gathering there. There were attempts to block internet links and of course, the official media was saying there were only 2,000 people at Tahrir. To a young woman, Mubarak was a "traitor." The best thing he could do, the only thing he should do, was "leave now." It was, very simply, a trust deficit of gigantic proportions.

There was a level of togetherness; even if they were different kinds of people, aware that if they were divided before a dictator, only the dustbin of history would be ready for them. You would see a whole crowd of people, sitting together around a fire in the middle of the night. When they weren't chanting slogans, or weren't marching from one side of the square to another, they were sitting around, waiting – waiting for their time, waiting for the dictator to go. You couldn't but admire their energy. In the middle of one night as President Mubarak finished his speech, saying he was ready to go, but in an orderly fashion in three months, not immediately, they protested. They wanted him to go immediately. They had waited 30 years; they couldn't wait another three months. They just couldn't imagine Mubarak for another three months. It was an offer they could refuse. Agitated demonstrators crowded around me as I entered Tahrir Square that night; resolute, overwhelmingly rejecting Mubarak's concession. "No having. We have no having," a group of obviously enraged and as a result, almost incoherent young men were saying. Again and again, crowds came before TV camera. "We want freedom. We want freedom," they said. When I asked people why they were so apprehensive about another three months of Mubarak, they worried about his strong-arm tactics. For one, he would arrest all those at Tahrir. "What did you do for Egypt in these 30 years? Nothing! So, why do you want another three months?" asked another protester.

There was a lot of talk especially in the West about the Muslim Brotherhood, about how radical they were. America was worried about the people at Tahrir, because American interests had been hurt after Iran 1979; there was little reason to look forward to another strategic ally heading down the lane of Islamic polity. However, while there were chants of "Allah o akbar" as expected in the Tahrir community, yet there wasn't much evidence of an undiluted hatred of America, only of Mubarak. If Obama supported Mubarak, if America supported Mubarak, they would be reviled but not otherwise. If the American government supported the protesters, it would be openly welcomed. From the protesters, there were very few references to Israel. It was all about Mubarak. Again and again, you heard people saying "Go Mubarak. Please go." Again and again, you saw posters against Mubarak. There was one of the last Pharaoh in his underpants—the Emperor has no clothes syndrome. Another one had a shocked-looking Mubarak being booted out by an exceptionally well-shod protestor. Whether they were wordy ("Wake up Mubarak, it's not a dream/ It's true, its real/ Justice and human rights are at the Door! /And there's no place for you any more" or as succinct as "Bollocks to you Mubarak. We hate you," they made the same point: Mubarak had to go.

It is not that there weren't worries about the Muslim Brotherhood in the West, a fear that they would Talibanise Egypt. A lot has been said about the Morsi government, but it hasn't been compared with Mullah Omar's. Even outside the Square, the unpopularity of the Mubarak government was evident. You asked a waiter in a restaurant, a staffer in your hotel, a taxi-driver about Mubarak and you would get a shake of the head. So, what was the alternative? Who would they favour? The answer was always "Muslim Brotherhood." First, the Brotherhood hasn't been a radical organisation. And secondly, at Tahrir, it wasn't just the Brotherhood. It was a national outpouring. How else can you explain this? However much he is a symbol of revolution over the last 40 years, would a Talibanised movement tolerate a poster of Che Guevara? "This is the big symbol of revolution around the world," said the man with the Che poster. There was too much poverty in Egypt, he said, too much "sickness." Mubarak has to go. He has to go, he said.

The more I think of Tahrir, the more I respect the people of Tahrir, particularly because it wasn't a very organised movement and because it was largely non-violent. Of course, there was fighting, but for all that, it was largely peaceful. I think the presence of children at the Square has much to do with it. And there were just so many children...fathers carrying flag-waving sons on their shoulders, little girls, ribbons in their hair, in the frontlines with their parents. Many people would be happy to die for a cause, but how many would sacrifice their children? How many would bring their children to a place if they know it was fraught with danger? How many people would have brickbats in one hand while they are holding on to their little boy or girl. I have one particular memory and it has stayed with me for years. Before the fighting, there was a little boy with a poster who used to come and stand beside me as I did my pieces to camera. He must have been about seven or eight. And as I looked up, I would see his father sitting a distance away with the boy's elder brother. He would smile and wave the Egyptian flag. I saw the boy the day the fighting began, the day Mubarak's armed goons in camels and horses slammed into the protesters. Several hundred people were injured in the fighting; I never saw the little boy after that. I don't know where he is—I really hope he is well.

Did anyone believe a menacing dictator would fade into the sunset? Does an iron-fisted ruler, deluded perhaps that he represented stability and that Egypt would descend into chaos once he departed, go without a last fight? It is almost surprising many didn't expect a last stand of the goons. It was the day after Mubarak's speech, his decision to resign in three months and the angry rebuff at Tahrir. After a long night and a longer morning, I was at the Hotel, Ramses Hilton, overlooking the Square when I got a call: Mubarak's supporters were moving towards Tahrir. Rushing out quickly, I found the Square a lot different from the way I left it an hour earlier. It comes from covering wars or riots or similar events: you get a feeling of impending trouble: that something's going to happen. Like me, people were streaming in from the Ramses Hilton side of Tahrir, all of them fit young men like the instructors you see at gyms, many of them were holding posters, most of them saying

"Mubarak good, El Baradei bad." I thought it almost Orwellian, which really shows where I personally stood on the issue, however objective I have to be for my channel.

There was going to be trouble. And I was on the phone doing a live that would never end, saying what it was looking like, that there was tension building up in the Square. One of Mubarak's men, and clearly the leader, saw me, he heard me speaking on the phone. I was telling viewers live what the posters Mubarak's men were carrying, the "Mubarak good, El Baradei bad" posters. He thought I was parroting their line and didn't bother me after that. I continued to be on the phone, saying again and again how dangerous it was getting and all it needed was a spark.

Then, came the spark. I could smell the camels and horses as they passed me, very, very close to me. If I had reached out, I could have touched them. Even on Mubarak's side, there were people who thought this was a bad idea. I heard one or two people saying "No, No," and caught the bridle of one or two animals and stopped them from going. But the others galloped towards the anti-Mubarak demonstrators on the other side of the Square, going straight into them. That's when (it was afternoon in Cairo, but evening in Delhi) – the fighting began. The anti-Mubarak faction hit back, throwing paving stones at them. From where I stood, after a few moments I saw a surge coming towards me, a moving sea of people. They were racing back, a crowd running away from the paving stones, the brickbats. I remember saying on air 'the sky is full of stones.' I was still on air describing what was going on to my viewers, and there would have been a lot of them, prime time approaching.

As the surge of people came closer and closer, I realised I had a choice. If I didn't want to get trampled, I would have to run, and run faster than the people behind me and that wasn't going to be easy if I were still on the phone, explaining to my viewers what I was seeing. A few metres away was a tank, an Egyptian army tank—there were many parked all around the Square, in fact, all over the city. I went and stood behind it. No one, I thought, would clamber over 40 tons of steel with a huge gun in the front and jump on me. I thought I was safe as people streamed past me. About half a minute later, I realised, my quick thinking had won me time—but about a minute at the best.

The paving stones, the bricks started to fall closer. I heard a PING first, and then, another PING and then, several more. That's the sound of paving stones when they fall on the steel turret of a tank. They were falling all around us. I was still on the phone of course, describing the paving stones falling. From behind me, Mubarak's men were doing the same—throwing paving stones. I realised I was caught in the middle of a riot and in serious danger of being hit. I knew I wasn't going to die, but a head injury in an alien city in the middle of a revolution didn't seem like a great idea.

One hit a man, in a white shirt on the head. He was standing close to me and his shirt quickly became red, soaked in blood. An elderly woman standing right beside me was panicking, screaming. Still on the phone, still telling my viewers what I was doing and what I was seeing, I decided I needed a bit more shelter. On my right, I noticed, was a burnt out truck; I crawled right under where the driver would have sat. I noticed I wasn't alone. There was a photographer there, a blond man, taking pictures. I still remember what he said to me. "Crouch," he said. "Just crouch," he kept saying. With good reason too, as you become a smaller target. The fighting seemed to go on and on. And then, I guess, people got a bit tired or ran out of stones. There was a lull in the fighting. It was also around the time my office felt I should find a way out of the Square and decided to end the marathon phono.

Looking around, I saw an exit out of Tahrir on my right. I quickly ran that side. An Egyptian army soldier was standing right at the gate. Seeing me in a black suit, and assuming I was respectable, probably wrongly, he quickly pulled me out and walked with me to a safer area. There was an Egyptian army colonel there and I remember having a chat with him. The army, of course, had not intervened. They had remained strictly neutral that day, a day one or two people were killed in the Square and an astonishing number—almost 800 injured, mostly head injuries.

Naturally, I would come back to the Square, do more reporting, but I was happy I wasn't a Western correspondent. Many of them were badly beaten up that afternoon by Mubarak's goons. I saw one man, I think he worked for a Western wire-service, being shoved against an armoured personnel carrier and beaten with a stick till a soldier intervened. It was a great advantage to be Indian. To look Western would have made me very conspicuous.

The results were evident the next morning. All the reporters would gather at the coffee shop of the Ramses Hilton during breakfast and we would see what had happened to whom. Many of the Western reporters had head injuries, or cuts or bruises. And of course, there was a famous anchor from an international channel. After the fighting began, he wouldn't leave his room and get to Tahrir. He would go live from his hotel room.

Street-fighting takes a lot out of streets. Walking to Tahrir the next day, through streets littered with brick-bats and other rubbish was an experience. It wasn't very different either. There was sporadic fighting; I remember there were a couple of gun-shots, but now, most journalists knew what to expect every morning. The resilience of the protestors at Tahrir must have been a lesson for the Mubarak regime. They realised they had played their last card—sending in goons to push the demonstrators out. And it hadn't worked. It was now a matter of time; the regime was on life-support. One day, there would be jubilation in Tahrir: Mubarak had gone, the regime had gone. The vigil was over.

3. Arab Women and the Arab Spring

Mary Totry

The World was overwhelmed by the Arab Spring triggered by a young Tunisian who set himself on fire on 17 December 2010. By the end of 2011 four autocratic regimes (Tunisia, Egypt, Libya and Yemen) had collapsed failing to confront the strong will and determination of their people. There were protests in Bahrain that were brutally crushed and protests in Jordan that were suppressed. The Syrian uprising that broke in 2011 and changed to a civil war has not come to an end yet.

In all these protests men and women alike (from all ages and backgrounds) went out to the street protesting against corruption, unemployment and police repression. In some countries, such as Tunisia and Egypt, women marched shoulder to shoulder with the men. In other countries such as Yemen, where sex segregation is the rule, women demonstrated alongside with men in parallel paths. Not only men did not oppose to women's participation in all of these protests, but they respected and supported women. Women were perceived then as equal comrades in a common battle towards freedom.

Women's participation in the Arab Spring was not unusual. Arab women have played a leading role in the long years of resistance to dictatorship in the Arab world, but during the Arab Spring they were unprecedentedly visible shattering the western stereotypes about them as being oppressed, marginalized and hidden behind the veil.

Although women played an essential role in the Arab Spring, they were marginalized once transition began. In some countries they were even turned against. No one had expected that the Islamic parties would take over in some of the countries, and no one could foresee the male gender constitution that developed later on. Women felt that they were let down by men they stood together with during the protests.[1] Many women activists expressed their fear that the victory of Islamic parties in the elections will undermine women's rights and force them out of the political arena. They believe that there is no difference between moderate Islamism and radical Islamists when it comes to social issues and citizens' rights that concern women. They also believe that dominant conservative value systems are being manipulated by religious discourse to deny women their rights.

In the last two years many people question whether the Arab Spring was a spring to Arab women too; whether it will devour the little hard-won rights that women achieved during the long years; whether women's participation in the protests was a guarantee to improve their status in societies and whether the resurgence of political Islam will negatively affect their rights. This paper will try to answer some of these questions focusing on two countries- Tunisia and Egypt as two different cases. While Tunisian women had maintained their rights and even gained some victories, Egyptian women suffered from regression after the revolution.

Women activists, bloggers, journalists, students and ordinary women were involved in every aspect of both revolutions. They confronted the security forces on the front line, organized protests, documented and informed the world about what was happening in their countries. They were active in writing slogans (Ben Ali, get out!) and enchanting them.[2] Women activists, like men activists, were arrested, detained, killed and tortured by the security forces. But they were also targets of additional forms of violence including sexual harassment, virginity tests,[3] abduction and rape. Nonetheless they continued bravely alongside with men in their fight to free their countries. Some of them were later on awarded for their significant role and extraordinary braveness. Tawakkol Karma from Yemen won the 2011 Nobel Prize for Peace. Asmaa Mahfouz from Egypt and Razan Zaitouneh from Syria were awarded the 2011 Sakharov prize.[4] Nawal Assadawi the Egyptian activist was graded sixteenth out of one hundred active people worldwide. Israa Abed El-Fattah[5] from Egypt was chosen among one hundred strong women in the world.

During the protests there was not a single slogan raised related to women's rights. Women as men demanded social justice, freedom, dignity, equality and democracy. Demands for equality between men and women were set aside. Women as men focused on bringing down the regime and dismantling oppressive state institutions. They believed that participating alongside with men will free their countries from repressive regimes and will automatically improve their status. Yet history teaches us that it is not always the case. Women's participation in the battle for freedom doesn't automatically guarantee equality. Women's rights are usually the first to be sacrificed by politicians seeking to hold on to power and to appease conservative factions.[6] In some countries hard won advances towards equal rights for women can be easily swept away like the case of Algeria after independence from the French Colonialism and the Yemeni case in the 1960s. In other countries like Iran a dictator fell from power, but a religious tyranny took its place and oppressed women.

To answer the questions raised earlier, I will present women's situation in politics prior and post the Tunisian and Egyptian revolutions; the legislative framework concerning women in both countries; the impact of Islamic parties on women's rights after the first elections; violence against women and the effect of the Arab Spring on women's awareness and orientation.

Women in Politics

Tunisian women were given the right to vote in 1957. Tunisian women's representation in the parliament and government prior and post the revolutions did not change much while there was a significant regression in Egyptian women's representation.

In 2009 Tunisian elections under Ben Ali's regime, 57 women were elected to the 214 seat house representing 27.6% of the Tunisian Parliament. In 2011 elections after Ben Ali, 57 women were elected to the 217 seat house representing 27.2% of the Tunisian Parliament. Tunisia is considered the second Arab country after Algeria[7] with the high representation of women in its parliament.

There was a slight decline in Tunisian women presentation in Government. While there were 4 women in the 45 member government

(8%) during Ben Ali's regime there were only 3 women in the 41 member cabinet (7%) following 2011 elections. Four out the six committees that prepared the new Tunisian constitution were headed by women.

Tunisian women were allowed to become judges since 1968. In 2011, women represented 27% of judges and 31% of lawyers. The level of education of Tunisian men and women are equal. Tunisian women are the majority in universities. Many of them hold decision-making positions in public and private sectors. Tunisian women didn't lose ground compared to women in other Arab countries.

Egypt was the first country in the Arab region (1956) to elect women for the People's Assembly- lower house. In 1979 Sadat introduced a quota of a minimum 30 seats for women in the parliament. At that time women represented only 9% of the parliament. In 2009 Mubarak enlarged women's quota to 64 seats. In 2010 elections under Mubarak's regime, 64 women were elected to the 382-seat Chamber, representing 13% of the Egyptian parliament. In May 2011 the Supreme Council of Armed Force (SCAF) abolished women's quota. As a result only 9 women were elected[8] and two women were appointed to the 508-seat People's Assembly, representing only 2% (a sharp drop from 13% prior the revolution).

There is also a Shura Council (the upper house) in Egypt that acts as an advisory capacity. Women were 4% of the Shura Council under Mubarak's regime and dropped to 2% after the revolution (4 out of 180 seats). There were 3 women in the 37 member government (8%) during Mubarak's regime and dropped to 2 women in the 31 member cabinet (7%) following 2011 elections under President Mursi.

The SCAF that took over power after Mubarak's resignation formed a Constitutional Committee that was supposed to draft a new constitution. Not a single woman was appointed to the Committee, although women were actively involved in the revolution.

In 2003 the first woman judge was appointed to the Supreme Constitutional Court by Mubarak, but was not allowed to hold hearings (up until then women were not allowed to be judges in Egypt). In 2007, thirty women judges were appointed to the civil courts. Nevertheless, women were not appointed to criminal courts or to the Office of the General Prosecutor on religious grounds.

The Legislative Framework

Egypt and Tunisia ratified CEDAW (*Convention to Eliminate All Forms of Discrimination against Women) in* 1981 and 1985 respectively, with reservations to several key provisions. While the Tunisian government announced to lift its reservations in August 2011, the Egyptian government refused to do so. As of March 2012 the withdrawal of the Tunisian government had not been formally registered with the UN. The reform of the Tunisian election law requiring parity on electoral lists represents a great victory to women, a first in the Arab region. The Egyptian government didn't agree to confirm the Amnesty International's proposal which is committed to basic human rights such as freedom of expression and assembly, religious freedom, non-discrimination and gender equality.[9]

The Tunisian Personal Code (1956) was considered advanced compared to other Personal Codes in the Arab World. It made adoption legal, abolished polygamy, conditioned concluding marriage with the consent of both spouses and gave equal access to divorce for both sexes. In the last decade a series of reforms were adopted in Tunisia to further strengthening the protection of women's right such as the Criminal Code 2004 which criminalize sexual harassment; the Personal Status Code 2007 which state that the minimum legal age for marriage for both sexes is 18; the 2008 law which strengthened the right to housing mothers with custody of minor children. Since 2010 mothers married to foreign men could transfer their nationalities to their children.

Nevertheless, many discriminatory provisions remain in force within the Tunisian Personal Code: the marriage of minors can be authorized in certain cases with the consent of the guardian and the mother; a dowry is required to conclude a marriage; Muslim women are not permitted to marry non-Muslims; the man remains the head of the family and bears the responsibility of providing for the family; women lose their children's custody when they remarry; men can retain custody if they have at their disposal a woman to take care of them; a woman can remarry only after three to four months while men can remarry immediately after divorce; women get half of amount of men's inheritance; the right of inheritance of non-Muslim women is limited. There is also discriminatory provision within the Penal Code which states that if the rapist is willing to marry his victim he can escape criminal persecution.

In the last decade a series of legislative reforms increased protection of several women's rights also in Egypt such as the new Child Law which rose the minimum age to eighteen for both sexes and other reforms in the Personal Status Law concerning divorce and child custody.

Despite reforms many discriminatory still exist: a male guardian is a must to conclude a marriage contract in Egypt; Urfi marriage is authorized (a man can destroy marriage documents and the woman can be accused to having sex outside marriage and be punished. He can also refuse to recognize his own children); a man can divorce his wife by saying "I repudiate you" three times and register the announcement within 30 days; women can file divorce only on certain grounds; since 2000 women can chose no-fault divorce (Khula procedure) but have to return the dowry and renounce all financial support; women can keep their children until the age of fifteen, they lose their children's custody when they remarry; a testimony of a man is equal to the testimony of two women in family courts; since 2000 women can travel freely without permission of their guardian, yet this freedom can be limited by court order; women get half of amount of men's inheritance; non-Muslim women married to Muslim men have no inheritance rights. The Nationality Law reformed in 2004 enabled women married to foreign men (not Palestinians) to grant nationality to their children. The Penal Code provides reduced sentences for men convicted of "honour killings" and free rapists who are willing to marry their victims. There is still no law criminalizing sexual harassment or domestic violence in Egypt.

Islamic Parties and their Impact on Women's Rights

Although Islamist parties won the Tunisian and Egyptian elections but their orientation towards women's issues is different. The Tunisian

Islamist party "Ennahda" won 41% of the seats among them many active women. "Ennahda" party proved that women can have a voice in decision-making processes. Although the party has stressed its commitment to maintaining the rights of women, there were some party representatives who made statements against women's right such as "Single mothers were a disgrace in an Arab Muslim society" or "Urfi marriage is a personal freedom". In October 2011 Channouchi, the head of "Ennahda" party, changed the adoption law. Unofficial segregation by sex started in universities and theatres. The Salafi activists wanted to impose the religious dress on women.

The Egyptian Islamist party "Freedom and Justice" won 47% of the seats and the Salafi "Al Nur" party won 24% making together 71% of the seats of the Egyptian parliament in 2012. Unlike the Tunisian "Ennahda" party the two Egyptian Islamist parties did not announce their commitment to maintain the rights of women. The "Freedom and Justice" has affirmed that a woman can't become a president and that only laws that agree with the Sharia are welcome. "Al Nur" party declined to promote women's rights or abolish the death penalty. Thus the majority of the Egyptian parliament was unwilling to be committed to promoting women's right and gender equality.

Not only were both Egyptian parties not committed to maintain women's right but some of their members were very hostile to women. Azza El Garf a parliament member from "Freedom and Justice" suggested abolishing the no-fault divorce (Khula) and objected to enacting a law criminalizing sexual harassment. She also demanded omitting the condition that the first wife should be informed of her husband's second wife. A Salafi member suggested permitting 12 year-old girls to marry. Salafi groups proposed abolishing the no-fault divorce (Khula) and repeal all laws contradicting with the Sharia. Since the revolution Islamists veiled women appear regularly on TV calling to enforce full veil on all Egyptian women.

The Egyptian public perception linked women's right to the propaganda of the former regime. Mubarak established "The National Council for Women" in 2000 headed by his wife. After the revolution, civil society organizations called for its dissolution. The SCAF did not dissolute it but nominated 30 new members. "Freedom and Justice" party contested its existence and demanded establishing a council for all members of the family. Women activists had to put their main energy trying to save what they had instead of trying to move forward with reform.

Violence Against Women

Violence against women existed before the two revolutions and continued after them. But the situation of Egyptian women got much worse than the Tunisian women. The later were sexually harassed and raped by Ben Ali's Special Forces during the protests. After the fall of Ben Ali women protesters were assaulted by groups of men shouting abusive statements and telling them "to return to their kitchen" (29 January 2011). Unveiled women suffered violence from Salafi group in the streets, but the government didn't immediately react. There were attacks on brothels, unveiled women teachers and students in the universities.

Violence against women is a major problem in Egypt. Women suffered from the brutality of Mubarak's regime but they were sexually harassed and assaulted after Mubarak resignation by the police and the military force. Following Mubarak's resignation and the transfer of power to the military forces, protesters continued to protest across the country criticizing the SCAF for not following their demands for reform. On 8 March 2011 hundreds of women gathered in Tahrir Square to mark International Women's Day and denounce their exclusion from decision-making process. Women were shouted "to return to their kitchen" and were sexually harassed by a group of Islamist young men. The next day 18 women protesters were severely beaten, tortured and verbally abused. Seven of them were forced to submit to virginity tests. On December 2011 Ghada Kamal was severely beaten and dragged half naked by soldiers. Four days later thousands of women participated in all-women march down-town Cairo protesting against the brutality of the army. Women activists who denounce gender discrimination had become targets of attacks. Nuhad Abu Kumsan the head for the Egyptian Centre for Women's Right, for example received a number of death threats. During June (2013) anti-Mursi protests ninety-one women were raped or sexually assaulted in public in Tahrir Square.

Egyptian women also suffer from sexual harassment and domestic violence that intensified after the revolution. There was a rise in criminal incidents against weak and disadvantaged groups, such as women, as a result of the chaos and loss of security characterizing most transition periods. According to a research[10] of representative sample 75% of women suffer from domestic violence, 41% suffer from physical violence (not from husbands). When women were asked about the reasons behind violence against them: 43% said it was the misinterpretation of religious concepts on women,[11] 39% said it was the patriarchal conservative tradition and 15% said the absence of laws defending women. Women believe that the retreat is a combination of the resurgence of patriarchal narrowly conservative social mores embedded in ancient tribal customs than with religion. Sharia, most of them think, is only a convenient peg for the deeper instinct of male dominance.

A report made by "The Egyptian Centre of Women's Rights" in 2012 showed an increase in violent incidents against women. Domestic violence was the major offence (59.4% of violent cases in the first six months after the revolution were "honour killing"). Rape is the second offence (every half an hour a female is raped in Egypt). Egypt was the second country in the world in sexual harassment before the revolution and became the first after the revolution. Many campaigns were set to fight the phenomenon. Women have become more vocal and are able to send abusers to court.

According to the Thomson Reuters Foundation poll[12] Egypt is considered the worst Arab state for women in 2013. The poll assessed six categories: violence against women, reproductive rights, treatment of women within the family, their integration into society and attitudes towards women's role in politics and the economy.

According to U.N. (2013) report 99.3% of women and girls were subjected to sexual harassment in Egypt. The social acceptability of everyday sexual harassment affects every woman in Egpyt regardless of age, professional or socio-economic background, marital status, dress or behaviour. It limits women's participation in public life and affects their safety and security, their sense of worth, self-confidence and health.

There was a rise in forced marriages and trafficking in women especially in villages on the outskirts of Cairo. Female genital mutilation has increased in recent years. According to UNICEF 91% of women and girls (27.2 million in all) in Egypt were subjected to mutilation.

Awareness of Women after the Arab Spring

Women realized that it was much easier to overthrow repressive regimes than to change the patriarchal narrowly conservative social mores embedded in ancient tribal customs. They also realized that this was a problem in all Arab countries and they have to unite efforts. In October 2011 four activists started a Facebook page under the title "I am with the Intifada of women in the Arab World" to give a platform for women from all Arab countries to speak openly about their suffering, demands and aspirations so that the all the world would know. The second aim of this initiative is to show the world that women's problem is not individual problems but rather social problems that should be solved. The Uprising will be fulfilled when women achieve their rights. They were united under the slogan "Together for free, independent and fearless women in the Arab world!"

Women activists said that the revolution had given women a voice and made a commitment that they who made the revolution alongside men will defend their rights and interests. The Arab spring has produced more grassroots youth activism whose equal access to social media tools is empowering individuals regardless of their gender or social class.

Conclusion

Although women have participated in the protests that led to the Region's transitions, they failed to protect their rights. Women hoped that they would be among prime beneficiaries of the Arab Spring, but they have instead been some of the biggest losers. Women's presence and participation in public life- especially in politics, decision-making positions and state affairs- moved from marginalization during repressive regimes to rejection with Islamist regimes. The revolutions have brought conflict, instability and a rise in Islamic groups. Still, in Tunisia the situation of women is not so bleak. Tunisian women continued to be active in the political process, because they had realized that they have the most to lose. Tunisian women have gained some victories.

The situation of Egyptian women had tremendously regressed. Although they played a central role in the revolution the rising influence of Islamists, culminating in the election of Muslim Brotherhood leader Mohamed Mursi as president was a major setback for women's rights. Even after he was toppled in a military takeover women still faced daily dangers on the street and in their homes. Women came to a conclusion that they need a double revolution, one against the dictators who ruined their countries and the other against a toxic mix of culture and religion that oppress them as women.

Notes

1. The Egyptian young men of the revolution did not include any woman in the revolution committee established after the revolution. Women felt they were equal in the protests but became second class citizens after the revolution.
2. http://www.youtube.com/watch?v=ld5NRuEkK1U
3. http://www.youtube.com/watch?v=c29CAXR141s
4. http://www.europarl.europa.eu/intcoop/sakharov/laureates/zaitouneh_en.html
5. She is called the Facebook girl. She co-founded the *April 6 Youth Movement Egypt* in 2008 and is an internet activist and blogger in Egypt.
6. The President of the Libyan National Transitional Council after announcing that Libya was liberated from Gaddafi, he announced that polygamy became legal. In doing so he made discrimination against Libyan women legal. The revised election Libyan law ignores women's role in ousting Gaddafi, it tries to eliminate women from politics and the revolution.
7. In the last election that was held in 2012 women won 31.38% of the Parliament seats in Algeria.
8. The elections were held between November 2011 and January 2012. The Muslim Brotherhood leader Mohamed Mursi was elected in June 2012 and was toppled in a military takeover in July 2013 after mass protests against his rule.
9. *FIDH/ Women and the Arab Spring: Taking Their Place?* March 2012
10. That was conducted by Alexandria Centre for Woman Health & Development.

11. Women have no brain and husbands have the right to discipline their wives.
12. The poll was conducted by 336 gender experts and ranked Egypt at the bottom of 22 Arab states.

4. Syria: the Last Secular Bastion in West Asia

Dr. Waiel Awwad

When the political assassination happened of the Tunisian activist, Chokri Belaid, the general coordinator of the Democratic Movement, it was an indication of commencement of the second phase of the Tunisian revolution, i.e. political assassination. The outrage was evident throughout Tunisia and the world, which had witnessed the birth of what was called the "Arab Spring", which in turn triggered a wave of unrest in most of the Arab capitals, toppled regimes, and is still simmering in many capitals and threatening to engulf others.

These ruthless killing, though happen to be a part of an ongoing process that began with the toppling of Zine Abidine Bin Ali regime. It exposed the true face of what claims to be "revolutionary guards" of political intolerance and strengthened the belief that this is not the alternative to that the people aspire for, and spilt the blood of innocent youth aspiring for a better life within a democratic set up. This is likely to have repercussions among the international community and well-wishers of the Arab peoples, which will lead to loss of sympathy for those who tried to hijack the true demands of the people.

The shock wave was strong enough to shake the establishments in neighboring countries, especially in Egypt among members of the opposition across the political spectrum. There was a justified fear that it may become the prototype for what could happen in Cairo very soon, especially after the declaration by a religious clergy calling for elimination of any opponent to president Morsi. The call was denounced and condemned by the vast majority of Egyptians.

In an interview given to *Al Khaleej* a few hours before his assassination, Chokri Belaid said among many other things, that the attack on Syria is a conspiracy and there is no revolution there.

The Rise of Arab Nationalism and The Plight of Arabs

In a sense, the roots of the Arab predicament lay in the transformation from feudal agricultural society to a modern industry society. After the fall of the Ottoman Empire, the Arab world had been carved up into small countries by Britain and France (Sykes-Picot Treaty) to firmly establish their influence and dominance. By the middle of the last century, when Europe was witnessing an internal conflict, the Arab countries gained independence and started political and economic reforms and inward restructuring to establish themselves as independent and sovereign nations. In the different capitals there took place, simultaneously, the birth of a pan-Arabism movement, which was challenged by the UK, France and USA who encouraged the nationalist forces in each country to thwart any project for Arab world unification which spreads from Qatar to Morocco.

In 1956 began what has come to be known as the Nasser Era, which witnessed in the consolidation of nationalist autocratic regimes across the Arab world. Many would blame the birth of Israel as a state at the cost of Palestine reinforced this tendency, but over the years it contributed to despair and resentment against the Arab governments, which failed to solve the conflict and give the Palestinians their legitimate right to establish a sovereign state in their homeland side by side with Israel and live in peace. In addition the discovery of oil and gas added to this rising tide of nationalism, where the Arab League helped in defining the contours of each Arab country within the borders delineated by the colonial powers namely France and Great Britain.

In the countries, however, that there was no oil reserve, there was a mass departure of human resources from the Arab world into US and Europe in search of a better future as unemployment ratio was very high 14.4% as compare to international figure of 6.3%. The tentative figure for such immigrants was put at 30 million in the 1990s and reached 100 million in 2009. Instead of being a force to reckon with, it became a burden on successful government and undermined the agenda of economic reforms.

Ironically, the population bomb turned out to be yet another challenge to confront the region. The population stood at 317 million in 2007 and is projected to rise up to 395 million by 2020. In other words, the Arab world would require nearly another 100 million new jobs – which drives home the urgency of success of economic reforms.

Further, the role of woman in the Arab world remains very limited. Only 33% of the Arab women participate in the economy, compared to 55% of the global figure. Their participation in political life was also limited and neglected in general.

Political reforms carried out in the Arab world were minimal and many political parties were barred, especially those with any Pan-Arabist agenda. People were allowed to gather only in mosques, which hardened the stands of those movements in the Arab world against any reconciliation with the ruling elites. In a curious way, this resulted in the belief that the responsibility for all the sufferings rested on the head of the state and his cronies, and hence poured their entire anger on the regimes and occasioned a call for a regime change.

Due to lack of political reforms and democratization in the Arab world, the regimes steadily declined in popularity. What complicated the matter more was the economic reforms associated with the new liberal economic policy, popularly known in the region as "King Lear Syndrome,"[1] which widened the gap between the rich and the poor and benefited only the creamy layers surrounding the leaders. The programme of reforms undertaken in the 1990s and the persistent lack of accountability fuelled more corruption, appeasement of vested interests, which in turn deepened lack of trust and anger among the people. The transformation of the orientation of the various economies towards liberal capitalism put a break on the possibilities of political liberalism; democratic elections were reduced to farcical and fruitless exercises that failed to create an indigenous alternative, which could have resulted in a more democratic polity and liberal culture.

The US interest in the Middle East

The Pan-Arab national movement witnessed a decline in the seventies which led to internal and regional conflicts and more divisions that kept the prospect of any development hanging on balance. This was followed by the two Gulf Wars. USA and the west focused on a "New Middle East &North African Order" and there is reason to suspect they went on to plot the changes the new order required. Their slogan was to promote human rights value, democracy, and civil societies and so on, to tie up the region under the American influence. In reality this agenda of "Reshaping the Middle East" started with the invasion of Iraq. Colin Powell stated this objective reasonably clearly: Washington was "[o] verdrawing the Middle East in ways that enhance the US interests and political landscape".

In fact James **Belen**, 1990, observed in the American Congress: "We need to ask our friends what we should do to topple regimes opposing the strategic interest of USA." Tariq Aziz ,the former foreign minister of Saddam`s regime, is on record saying that after pushing Iraq into a war with Iran for 8 years that left more than a million dead on either side and extensive damages and losses, the White House encouraged the Iraqi regime was to occupy Kuwait.

Despite the resentment against the Iraqi regime, the US invasion to Iraq led to more anger in the Arab streets which was aggravated by the global financial crisis, economic recession and the rise in price of essential commodities. The youth in the Arab street, fed up with the policy of puppet regimes, that did not carry much of reforms to meet the minimum requirement decided to take the law into their hands and get rid of those regimes that suppressed them and denied them their basic rights.

"The Arab Spring"

The turmoil in the Arab street in the 21st century, the so-called "Arab Spring" is a reflection of the anger with which the Arab middle class is seething. It has been piling up for decades, which was ignored by the ruling elite regardless of whether it was republican form of government, or a monarchy. For long, the innocent bystander had falsely been briefed about the achievements of the ruler/ruling elite, much to the appreciation of "rented mass" supporting such policy. But of late, all the various strata of the society have joined in to express their angers and sufferings that have been piling over the years. Some analysts have chosen to call it a less secular revolution which has taken place in Tunisia; others have added economic and political angles to the revolt in Egypt where the people had been kept at bay from the decision making of the government in matters which directly affected their daily livelihood.

What is more astonishing is the quick success of these peaceful disturbances that toppled regimes, which one could never have dreamed as possible before 2011. Eschewing egoism, sectarian and individualism, people were happy to express their feelings about their rulers without fear. They formed peoples committees, opened dialogue with the military, and adhered to legitimate demands like political freedom, free election, new constitution, economic development and social justice -- all being perfectly legitimate demands.

Despite the war propaganda and the massive diplomatic offensive by the West and US to justify the invasion of Iraq in 2003 by the US and UK, the vast majority of the international community was of the belief that the reason behind the invasion was the thirst for Iraq's oil and natural resources. The true motive had never been the WMD, (Weapon of Mass Destruction); it was a campaign was essentially operationalised by a Weapon of Mass deception.

The true nature of occupation and its outcome were quite obvious, because the US and its allies never were interested in bringing democracy to West Asia but chaos and destruction. A total anarchy that will ensure hegemony of the great power in the new game played out since 2010 under the pretext of what is called the "Arab Spring". The onset of the unrest was done after an agreement between the US, Turkey and Muslim Brotherhood Organization in Ankara in 2009. In accordance with this deal, the MB was allowed to take over the Arab regimes provided the American and Israel interests continue to be safeguarded in the region. Washington was leading quietly a war in the region to define its role in the third millennium in globe and in a region rich of natural resources in an era of global economic recession, financial crisis, and bankrupted Europe.

Targeting Syria

Syria occupies a strategic location in the Middle East. It is considered the cradle of civilization which goes back to the Bronze Age because of its fertile land. It is a heterogeneous society with a majority of Arabs and a multi linguistic society: the people speak Arabic, Armenian, Kurdish and Assyrian, and Aramaic, (the oldest language (of Jesus Christ) is still spoken in Syria in small villages like Maalloula, Jabaadin and Bakhaa and many other areas of Christian dominated areas) over and above French.

When USA invaded Iraq, US General Colin Powell, paid a visit to Syria carrying a list of demands for Damascus which included: ending of Syria-Iran alliance; withdrawal of forces from Lebanon; dismantling the Hezbollah, stopping of the support to Hamas and opening up of Syrian market, etc. Damascus gave a cold shoulder to Mr. Powell, and the plot presumably began to thicken against Syria which was to come after Iraq. Former NATO Director General Wesley Clark said in 2007 about the Neocons plan`s, that NATO is planning to occupy 7 countries in five years including Libya, Yemen, Somalia, Sudan, Syria and Iran. Even Wikileaks revealed the US plan to a military coup in Tunisia and Egypt to gain logistic support to invade Libya. Now Al Qaeda in North Africa is gaining ground to take on Algeria.

The drawing of the map of new Middle East and North Africa is meant to divide the region into small countries on ethnic and religious basis. The Islamic parties gaining power in most of the Arab states went for election from Morocco, Tunisia, Libya and Egypt. Many have accused Qatar and Saudi Arabia of pumping billions of dollars to let the Islamist parties gain control. This position is fuelled by the general perception that the departure of US from Iraq will lead to a vacuum, and the growing regional power of Iran will fill this vacuum, thereby strengthening the resistance against Israeli occupation. The Shi‘i powers of Iran, Iraq and Syria will be a threat to the US-Israeli strategic partnership. By toppling the regime in Syria, the West in general and the US in particular believes Iran will lose a strong ally in the region, and will be more isolated. This in turn would lead to a defeat of the Lebanese Hezbollah. By contrast Russia feels that the fall of Syria will widen the influence of the Sunni Islamists in the region and will be a part of the containment plan against Iran by the US and the West.

The new maps of the Middle East were drawn by US scholars and military experts and published in military journals and books.[2] The work details how tarnishing of the image of USA was tarnished in the Arab world, which led to a program set up by the Neocons, who were advocating "the New Middle East Order", to glorify the American image in the eyes of the masses. Millions of Dollars were spent on social networking, media institutions and many were on the payrolls of the CIA, programs were launched in the US and Arab youths were invited to attend seminars and trained on networking, and how to organize protests and lead demonstrations to meet the aspirations of the people, and hence insure a "regime change" to meet the socio-economic demands in countries infested with malpractice of unchallengeable regimes, lack of democracy, unemployment, poverty, illiteracy, fanaticism and sectarian divide.

The "Constructive Chaos" project for the Arab world can be said to have begun with the Balkanization in Sudan, which was divided into two; regimes were overthrown in Tunisia and Egypt but the eye was on Libya, which was attacked by France at the head of the NATO forces under the rubric of "Humanitarian Intervention", that compounded the problems and prompted other super powers to prevent similar action in other country like Syria. In fact even Silvia Berlusconi the former prime minister of Italy accused France`s President Sarkozy of initiating a war on Gaddafi who was loved by his people, on the request of his friend Bernard Livy Henry, even though Libya was peaceful and there was no revolt against the Libyan president .[3]

War on Syria

The winds of change which started in Tunisia and Egypt reached Syrian shores sooner than expected since the general perception was the revolts were against pro-Western regimes. But the common ground was the same internally in respect to economic and political reforms in the Arab World, which led people to spell out their angers in the streets to cause the changes. The Syrian President formed a committee to study the reasons that led to the uprising and changes in Tunisia and Egypt and tried to enhance political and economic reforms to meet the aspiration of the people. But as we say in Arabic "The winds do not blow as the vessel wishes". Syria was caught unaware of the plot planned for her from neighboring countries, and is still struggling to calm down the streets and eliminate the militant groups, the armed infiltrators. The insurgents took the advantage of the genuine demands of the demonstrators and tried to settle scores with Syrian regime either to topple it, or correct its track as per the wishes of US and the West in regards to regional issue, with an eye to eventually peace with Israel and isolating Iran.

The opposition movement was largely peaceful which ignited in Deraa, a city to the south of Damascus. From day one, it was meant to topple the regime because whatever demands made by the insurgents was conceded by the government met with objection. This was quickly discernible by Syrians, especially when slogans like "No Iran No Hezbollah", "We Want a president who fears Allah" were raised in Daraa city. It is an indication that the ulterior objective behind the uprising happens to be inciting the people along lines of sectarian strife rather than a triggering a genuine revolt for economic and political reforms. It was repeated in different parts of Syria viz. Talkalakh, Jisr Alshougor, Idlib, Aleppo and Homs. As Syria continues to bleed and continues to hold out, at least 150,000 mercenaries from 83 nations are fighting the Syrian government forces, supported by the EU, regional players and monarchs.

William Blum in his book, *US Military and CIA Interventions since World War II*, spoke about the US and CIA military intervention: invasions … bombings … overthrowing governments … occupations … suppressing movements for social change … assassinating political leaders … perverting elections … manipulating labor unions …

manufacturing news ... economic and political sanctions ... death squads ...torture ... biological warfare ... depleted uranium ...drug trafficking ... mercenaries. For the US to wage a war is more important and profitable than winning it. Recent reports from US media suggest that the law makers in the US are investing their money in the arms industry and making millions of dollars in profits from waging wars while American taxpayers have to bear the cost of wars in Afghanistan, Iraq and Pakistan. Between 2001 and 2005 defense corporations' annual profits climbed 189%. It is the military establishment in the US which is dictating the foreign policy, specially the foreign policy that keeps US at war.[4] In 1819 February18, US Congress rejected the rule of law in foreign policy (Seminole War) and ever since the rule of force was established as a major drive in foreign policy as much as religious belief.[5]

With money and arms, trained "Jihadists" are turning Syria into a heaven for extremists. Reports from Ankara suggest that thousands of Libyan Zentan tribe, Chechens, Turkoman, Tunisians, Pakistanis, Saudis are trained on the border for 3 weeks, given a gun and 'the key to heaven' before sending him to Syria to fight the "Infidel regime" represented by Bashar al-Assad. Earlier on it was a mixed group of people from different strata of the society who wanted to achieve a change in the ruling system and allow more freedom, social justice and equality in a democratic system.

Gradually, with arming the rebels the streets became fragmented into different forces which dominate the unrest. Chief among these are 1) Islamist Jihadists of Wahhabi/Salafi persuasion, equipped with money and authority. Funded and supported by Qatar, Saudi Arabia and blessed by the USA, they are anti-Shi'i in their orientation. They are ready to kill a third of the nation for the remaining two thirds (.i.e 8 million religious minorities for the sake of 16 million Sunnis). 2) The modernized Muslim Brotherhood, which enjoys the support of Turkey, USA and the West. They are determined to avenge the bloody suppression of 1982. They have popularized the slogan "If Mubarak was toppled because of Facebook, you are because of Abook (your father)." 3) the Moderate movement, comprising of nationalists, Pan-

Arabists, resistance left, liberal and neo liberal forces supported by Iran and fighting hegemony of the West. Currently, this is the weakest. It lacks finances, media coverage and strong base. 4) Secular forces with little or no external support. Most of the secular forces pulled out of the demonstration as violence reached new heights, and the government began to give in to their demands and got ready for reforms. The Jihadist forces have now become the prominent force which the Syrian regime is fighting on different fronts

Type of War in Syria:

The war on Syria escalated in 2013 and more trained terrorists were sent from different countries who found shelters among dissents groups. Mobilising local recruits became easier with hardship on account of economic sanctions and lack of essential medicine. Reports from northern Syria reveal that the Islamist militants are forcing people to join their ranks, implement strict Islamic roles in exchange of bread and butter stolen from government and private stores.

The war on Syria is bound to be prolonged, particularly as the government has drawn a plan to fight on different fronts simultaneously. The fight, however, becomes more of defensive and existential where the government forces engaged with Jihadists and foreign mercenaries belonging to Muslim Brotherhood, Salafists and Wahabbi affiliation. Defensive and influenced where it is facing secularists with minimal compromise.

According to Lebanese paper Alakhbar, a model was established known as **The Belhaj Model.** It says:

> "Islamist insiders today insist that the key group in the movement today is the Ahrar al-Sham Brigades and not the Nusra Front, which receives the most attention. They argue that the leadership of the Ahrar Brigades, after its merger with a number of other Islamists factions over the summer, is the one that is guiding the movement, particularly on the ideological level. To this end, the movement has produced a 40-page internal manifesto to organize and direct its members. The

document emulates the experience of Abdul-Hakim Belhaj, the Libyan Islamist rebel leader, borrowing the following four points:

- The call for jihad must be waged under the banner of Islam.
- Islamic law is to be enforced by setting up specialized councils in the various locales, whose duty it is to apply the law on civilians and combatants alike. News has been circulating recently that a supreme council has also been formed to appoint and oversee the work of local ones.
- The goal is to establish a state in Syria that is not necessarily religious, with the proviso that it is not based on the military and that it implements Islamic law based on the idea that it is the will of the majority.
- With the toppling of the regime, the military brigades must dissolve themselves and surrender their weapons to the newly established armed forces, integrating competent fighters into the new Syrian army."

After the success of Syrian forces in defeating the militants groups in different parts of Syria , Saudi Arabia stepped in to unite the radical groups under one banner to defeat the Syrian army and hold some ground before going to the negotiating table .

The emergence of Islamic state of Iraq and Sham (Daash /ISIS),led to the takeover of most of the troops from the northern part of Syria from the so called "Free Syria Army"(FSA) and declaring loyalty to Al Qaeda. USA and UK suspended the arm supplies to FSA after the ISIS confiscated the weapons stored by the FSA .

Syria's Foes and Allies

In spite of the amount of killings and destructions the government still has the advantage of the support from the army, and the vast majority of Syrians who spurn the horrendous crimes carried out by those extremists in the name of Islam. In this battle, Syrian regimes success in standing its own ground has depended on some of its allies such as Russia and Iran.

The Russian position in support of president Assad is based on the principle of, and determination not to, let the US and NATO allies turn Syria into another Libya. This support flows directly driven by national interest, because the fear of being engulfed by Islamists and extremists spread from North Africa and Turkey which will have a repercussion on its own minorities. The other important reason is the gas pipelines to Europe and the attempt by US and Qatar to extend pipelines through Syria to Europe to reduce the dependence of the later on the Russian `s gas. Additionally, one has to bear in mind the discovery of gas in the Mediterranean and want its share of it.

Iran and Syria enjoy a strategic relationship ever since the Islamic revolution, ending the era of Iran as the policeman state of US interest in the region. This strategic relationship consolidated throughout the decades which strengthened the resistance bloc against US-Israel hegemony.

India as a leader of the BRICS took a firm stand for a peaceful solution by the Syrians and the international community should facilitate the dialogue and put an end to violence from both sides. China despite all the lucrative incentives from the gulf refused to budge and committed to the policy of non interferences based on UN charter. Many other countries stood with Syria in its fight against the terrorist war imposed on it like Algeria, Sudan, Lebanon, South Africa, Brazil, Cuba and Venezuela to name a few.

Among its adversaries, Damascus stares at a growing combination between USA, Turkey and Israrel. US interference in the internal affairs of Syria goes back to 1949 were they helped and assessed Hosni Alzaim to topple the first democratically elected government led by Shekri Alkuwatly. Even the giant media houses have played their role in the war on Syria, and there has been no let up till date. Headlines like : "West needs Syria in turmoil", "Israel see Assad lesser Evil", "Reshaping the Middle East", "How to topple Assad" , "How to surpass Russia and China`s veto", "post Assad Scenario" and so on so forth. Not a single country spoke how to save Syria from a war or even engage the Syrian government to find a solution to the crisis. When the US secretary of state Hillary Clinton called the Chinese and Russian veto of UN Syrian resolution "despicable", the Chinese questioned the American morality of protecting the Arabs while the whole world still remember Abu Ghraib prison in Iraq and using of Phosphorus bombs in Fallujah city of Iraq of Sunni majority which flattened the city. Not to speak of NATO war on Libya and post Qaddafi civil war or even to speak of the latest incidence of burning copies of the holy book by US soldiers in Afghanistan.

Israel never hid its intention toward disintegration of Syria and widely published the plan how Syria should be divided.[6] In regards to Syria the plan stated:" The Western front, which on the surface appears more problematic, is in fact less complicated than the Eastern front, in which most of the events that make the headlines have been taking place recently. Lebanon's total dissolution *into five provinces serves as a precedent for the entire Arab world including Egypt, Syria, Iraq and the Arabian peninsula and is already following that track. The dissolution of Syria and Iraq later on into ethnically or religiously unique areas such as in Lebanon, is Israel's primary target on the Eastern front in the long run, while the dissolution of the military power of those states serves as the primary short term target. Syria will fall apart, in accordance with its ethnic and religious structure, into several states such as in present day Lebanon, so that there will be a Shi'ite Alawi state along its coast, a Sunni state in the Aleppo area, another Sunni state in Damascus hostile to its northern neighbor, and the Druzes who will set up a state*, maybe even in our Golan, and certainly in the Hauran and *in northern Jordan.* This state of affairs will be the guarantee for peace and security in the area in the long run, *and that aim is already within our reach today."*

The naked aggression and provocative attacks by Israel Military on a scientific research centre in outskirt of Damascus met with wide condemnation and considered as a crime, an act of terrorism, opening a new front and assisting the rebels who failed to achieve its objectives on the ground.

The talk of creating a Buffer Zone inside Syria, strengthened the belief among Syrians that Israel in the sole beneficiary of the current unrest in Syria.[7]

Turkey on the other hand, besides being a NATO ally, has very close ties with Israel and US. The current government enjoyed the best relation with Syria; its business flourished, cross borders trade and visa regime was eased leading to considerable benefit of trade (more than 6 billion USD annually for Turkey). Syrian industry faced harsh time after the surplus from Turkey and went into huge loss with more employees losing their daily wages.

President Assad declined repeated insistence from Ankara to share power with Muslim Brotherhood and give them one third of seats in the cabinet. Assad told his Turkish counterpart that Syrian constitution is a secular one and does not allow religious party but they can contest election as individual. This angered Erdogan and the rest is known. The war on Syria cost Turkey dearly and Damascus accused Ankara of stealing and destroying factories in Syria, dismantling more than 1500 factories in Aleppo alone, the commercial capital, sold at a token price by the rebels. Evidences are widely available on YouTube about the transportation of equipment to Turkey.[8]

The Islamic insurgency has been gaining ground in Syria with the influx of mercenaries equipped with sophisticated arms (M79 Osa rocket launcher, the RPG-22, the M-60 recoilless rifle and the RBG-6 multiple grenade launcher, Austrian Steyr Aug rifles) and ammunition, trained and supervised by CIA, Mossad, MI5, the French intelligence along with the support of Qatar and the Saudis trying to overpower the prevailing order. The widespread of networking and coordination among insurgent groups with the help of sophisticated telecommunication system provided by France and USA, they were able to spread all over Syria under different names and commands.[9] Chief among these are: the ISIS (an al-Qaeda affiliated group, the backbone of resistance to the Assad regime); Jabhat Al Nusra (mainly foreign Islamists linked to Al Qaeda specializing in suicidal operation, executions and training for fresh recruits); Kataib Ahrar Al Sham Al-Islamiah (made of around 50 Jihadi groups which form the Syria Islamic Front).[10] They are Islamic in nature because it is easy to recruits extremists along the line of sectarian divides. Additionally, foreign support is easily available from rich Gulf States and Islamic organizations. But most importantly because President Assad's regional policy made more enemies than among the Islamist powers.

Conclusion

The spread of terrorism in the region has become so evident that the international community can not ignore any longer the prospect of spreading the conflict to neighboring countries and an all out war that will threaten the global peace and stability. Besides, there came the acknowledgement that this war will not be able to topple the Syrian government, and hence political de-escalation was seen in course of 2013. A peaceful solution may even be achievable in the Geneva summit of January 2014. But without cutting the funds and arm, the Syrian blood will continue to be spilt and the Syrian front will remain a battle ground for a proxy war between the superpowers .

In spite of the bloody path in Syria and the engagement of the Syrian army in fighting, President Assad has gone ahead with political and economical reforms and announced a road map that will ensure establishing of a wider base for democratization of Syria. Washington, in a way did a diplomatic volte-face on Syria and nodded for the Geneva Accords. If USA finally accepts President Assad's plan in the forthcoming Summit with Russia, then it will set up the stage for a political solution to the Syrian crisis. Otherwise the Syrian conflict could degenerate into an all-out war in the region, while the Syrian government continues to restore law and order in the state and protect its population from terrorist organizations.

Notes

1. Roger Owen, the Rise and Fall of Arab Presidents for Life "(page121),
2. retired Lieutenant-Colonel's book, Never Quit the Fight, and Blood Borders: How a better Middle East would look, in the U.S. military's Armed Forces Journal with commentary from Ralph Peters
3. http://www.dailymotion.com/video/xhdrv8_l-appel-de-bhl-depuis-benghazi-libye-en-direct-sur-tf1-au_news#.UPOateTBjFk
4. http://www.brasschecktv.com/videos/war-is-a-racket/foreign-policy-and-war-profiteering-.html

5. *Sword of the Spirit, Shield of Faith: Religion in American War and Diplomacy.*
6. Oded Yinon, "A Strategy for Israel in the Nineteen Eighties" , (tr. by Israel Shahak), This essay originally appeared in Hebrew in KIVUNIM (Directions), *A Journal for Judaism and Zionism*; Issue No, 14--Winter, 5742, February 1982. Published by the Department of Publicity/The World Zionist Organization, Jerusalem.
7. "Israeli Aggression Reveals Israel's Role in Destabilizing Syria.", Syrian Arab News Agency, 3rd February, 2013.
8. http://www.youtube.com/watch?v=i9uWKVjY3a4
9. Aaron Lund, "Syrian Jihadism" UL Brief no. 13, published by Swedish Institute of International Affairs, 14 September 2013, http://www.ui.se/upl/files/77409.pdf
10. There are several more splinter outfits, such as the Soquor Al Sham (Active in Lattakia ,Jabal Alzawiah); Liwa Al Tawhid (Damacus); Harakat Al Fajr Al Islamia (Aleppo and neighboring areas); Kataib Ansar AlSham (Lattakia, Homs); Soquor Al-Islam (Damascus); Kataib al Imam Al muqatila (Damascus); Katibat Hamza Bin AbdulMuttalib (Damascus –Zabadani resort area); Liwa Alhaq; Kataib Al Farooq (Homs); Katibat Musab Bin Omair (Rural Aleppo); (Jamat Altaleea :Idlib); Jaish Altawhid (Deir Elzour); Jabhat Tahrir; Jabhat Alasala wa Al tanmiah; Tajamou Ansar Al-Islam fi Qalb Alsham; Liwa Ahfad Alrasoul; Liwa al-Islam: (Damascus); Salafi Syria Islamic Front (Eljabha Elislamiah ElSouriah) formed by Ahrar Al-Sham; Fateh Al-Islam (Funded by Lebanese Islamist groups and Gulf States); Amouminoun Yusharikon : (Salafist ,active in Deraa); Firkat Sulieman Al Mukatilah (Hama); Abdula Azam ,Fajr Al Islam and many of these groups and small factions are fighting under Syria Liberation Front.

5. The Interplay between Identity and Sovereignty of Middle Eastern States in Light of the Arab Uprisings: the case of Lebanon

Joseph Alagha

Abstract

Are the Arabs still in the phase of state building? Did the Arab Uprisings fail? Is the problem in the transition from autocracy to democratic rule? Alternatively, does it have to do with the dilemma of popular sovereignty and institutionalism? What is the relationship between identity and state sovereignty? What is the role of post-Islamism in this regard? What is the impact of the US and regional actors, both the core Arab states and the peripheral non-Arab states of Israel, Turkey, and Iran? This paper endeavours to address these dynamics in light of the challenges facing the liberalisation and democratisation processes in the Middle East and North Africa (MENA) region, where the Arab Uprisings seem to have no ideology, no unified leadership, and hardly resulted in institutionalisation and constitutionalism.

Sovereignty to the People: an Impossible Task?

Which sovereignty to the people are we talking about in the Middle East if the populace were always subdued by the hegemonic power? Four hundred years of Ottoman rule from 1516 to 1918, were followed by harsh colonisation (1916 Sykes-Picot),[1] then the reign of terror of the autocratic regimes (which came about through coup d'état) and intelligence states. Within these overwhelming conditions, people could not vent their anger; rather, they were almost always contained and crushed. It was not until the so-called 'Arab Spring' or the 2010-11 Arab Uprisings that allowed the masses to vent their anger and shout: 'The people want to change the regime'. It seems that the Arab countries are still struggling with the notion and concept of state building. Overall, I argue that the Arab Spring constitutes a movement towards liberalisation and democratisation in its essence and orientation, but it lacks many credentials and ingredients of Western theories of democracy and societal transformation. From a neo-realist perspective, I begin with a theoretical background in order to map the interplay between identity and state sovereignty in relation to the concept of popular sovereignty. Abraham Lincoln understood democracy as popular sovereignty: "Government for the people, to the people, and by the people", i.e. sovereignty should be vested in the (hands of) people, not dictators. So did Thomas Jefferson: "If it were up to me to have government without press or press without government, I would not hesitate a moment to choose the latter". Similar unwavering commitment to the freedom of press, speech, expression, social justice, and dignity of the people, formed the backbone of the Arab Spring's call of 'The people want to topple the regime'.

Theoretical Framework

I start by defining 'idealist', 'utopianism or idealism', and 'realism'. An idealist is "one who sees such values or human preferences as justice or a desire for world peace as potentially decisive and capable of overcoming obstacles to their realization. Referred to by critics as *utopian*, in that the idealist does not understand the realities that constrain human choice. An idealist considers ideas as having important causal effects as opposed to others who see power or material factors as being the determinants of political outcomes".[2] Utopianism or idealism is "a tradition of political thought [ideology] that emphasizes what unites peoples...[It is] the opposite of, *realism* in foreign policy, which focuses primarily on national interests and power considerations. This rigid idealist-realist dichotomy can be misleading, however, since many realists also incorporate value considerations in their analyses and prescriptions"[3]

[The Lebanese Islamic movement Hizbullah endeavours to incorporate elements of its political ideology in its political program]. Realism is a "traditionally dominant school of international relations theory. States are seen as unitary rational actors advancing their national interests amidst the insecurity of the anarchic international arena. International politics is a struggle for power, war is an ever-present possibility, and order depends on a balance of power. Decision maker rationality means careful 'realistic' matching of goals and resources (the commonsense use of the world *realism*)".[4]

The claims of realism that Hinnebusch assumes are set as follows. First, the state is the main actor in foreign policy, and thus the elites of the state have an "... interest in maximizing the autonomy and security of the state".[5] Second, it accepts that anarchy is an inherent feature of the international system that generates "... profound insecurity and pervasive struggle for power", even more so in the Middle East.[6] The third assumption is that states seek to counter these menaces "... through 'reason of state', notably power accumulation and balancing, and that the latter is a key to the regional order".[7] However, realism incurs many disadvantages in understanding the Middle East.

Concerning the juncture of identity and sovereignty that has become one of the chief tenets to challenge the superiority of realism in explaining international relations, Hinnebusch is open to discuss themes that a well respected realist is to leave behind as questions more properly concerning the analysts of political life inside the state: "The unique feature of the Middle East state system, specifically the uneasy relation of identity and state sovereignty, immensely complicate foreign policymaking in the Middle East. The realist model, in which elites represent loyal populations insulated from external influence in the conduct of foreign policy, must be substantially modified in analysis of the region".[8]

The substantial modification in Hinnebusch's view is that many Middle Eastern states lack "impermeability and secure national identity-—that realism assumes".[9] Moreover, "loyalty to the individual states is contested by substate and suprastate identities. The resultant embedding of the state system in a matrix of fluid multiple identities means that the 'national interest' that realism assumes underlies foreign policy is problematic and contested".[10] Therefore, "built-in" anomalies of irredentist tendencies are characteristic of the region. They are reflected in the expression of the practices and worldviews of various ethnic and religious milieus, which challenge the immutability of territorial borders, thus simulating territorial conflict between states. Added to this is the immense and complicated power that Islam possesses as a trans-national, suprastate identity, which structures and commands the lives and worldviews of the people in the region. This makes the resort to the juncture of political identity and state sovereignty legitimate and wanting. Thus, the generated duality, which the ruling elite have to grapple with between asserting *raison de la nation* (pan-Arabism/pan-Islamism) and *raison d'etat* (state sovereignty), is what has compelled them to treat the region as an arena of trans-state political competition.

According to Michael Barnett's constructivist theory, identity is constructed; it is never monolithic and given, rather identities in the Middle East are contested, complex, and multiple. Identity is something that is shaped and moulded by the historical experience and interaction of leaders and nations. As Hinnebusch puts it, "The interaction of leaders also 'deconstructed' Pan-Arabism, so to speak: interstate disagreement over its meaning and the failures of Arab unity projects and of Arab collective institutions disillusioned and demobilized Arab publics, reducing Pan-Arab constraints on state leaders".[11] Hinnebusch gives two main reasons why these identities have declined. Firstly, he points to the neglect of power by constructivists who fail to see that it is military power, and not public opinion that was responsible in leading the state to put self-help over identity. Secondly, residual Pan-Arabism still continues to have an impact on foreign policymaking since state identities are no good substitute for that matter. Thus, the problem of legitimacy is partially resolved by recourse to Pan-Arabism or Pan-Islamism as a contingency measure to disguise, justify, and sometimes modify the reason of state.[12]

According to Shibley Telhami and Michael Barnett, "Constructivism posits that social (and international) structures are alloyed with normative [ideological] and material elements, that social structures constitute actors' identities and interests, and that the practices of actors embedded in the social structure not only reproduce the structure but also sometimes transform it".[13] Joshua Goldstein adds that constructivists seek to better understand world politics by listening to voices silenced by power, for instance, the voices of oppressed ethnic minorities.[14] Michael Barnett defines collective (social) identity as: " 'An identity is the understanding of oneself in relation to others'. Identity is inherently relational—one defines oneself or groups define themselves in part by who belongs and, as important, by who does not belong".[15] Linking identity to ideology, Telhami and Barnett argue, "Identity appears most prominently as an ideological device to justify self-interested politics [Identity] makes some action legitimate and intelligible and others not so".[16] According to Alexander Wendt, social identities are "identities that political actors generate through interaction with other actors".[17] How do these theoretical considerations relate to the Lebanese Hizbullah?

Theoretical Application

Hinnebusch's three Levels and the Dynamic between Identity and State Sovereignty

I employ Hinnebusch's "three conceptually distinct environments", which distinguish among the "domestic level", the "regional systematic level", and the "global (or international) level".[18] In Hizbullah's case, the domestic level corresponds to Lebanon; the regional level comprises Israel/Palestine, Syria, and Iran; and the international level, in addition to pan-Islamism, refers to Hizbullah's stance towards the US and Europe. This is done in order to study why and how the three levels or environments effect Hizbullah's identity construction. In this respect, Hinnebusch argues, "Constructivists insist that interstate relations are contingent on the way identity is constructed; in the Middle East, sub- and suprastate identities compete with state identity, inspire trans-state movements [transnational Islamic movements such as Hizbullah], and constrain purely state-centric behaviour."[19] In a similar vein, Telhami and Barnett state that constructivism considers "that identity essentially constructs the world so that perceptions of one's state and others are defined by one's identity."[20] Likening this to resource mobilization, internationally and regionally, Hinnebusch argues that in the Middle East, "populations have remained mobilizable by transstate and irredentist[21] ideology".[22] In this perspective, the effect of the Islamic Revolution's ideology is clearly salient on Hizbullah's ideology and identity. Domestically, Hinnebusch comes out with the following hypothesis: "the more the state system thwarted indigenous interests and identity [Shi'ite interests and Hizbullah's identity], the more status quo social forces inside the states were weakened [for instance, the Christian Lebanese Forces and Sunni political parties] and the more radical, middle class, or even plebeian forces were mobilized [for example, the Hizbullahis]".[23]

Since Hinnebusch based his argument on the distinction between identity and state sovereignty[24], an important challenge is to study and evaluate the dynamic between Hizbullah's Islamist identity and Lebanese state sovereignty. According to Hinnebusch, "the unique feature of the Middle East state system, specifically the uneasy relation of identity and state sovereignty, immensely complicate foreign policymaking in the Middle East...[because] Middle Eastern states lack impermeability and secure national identity".[25] Moreover, Hinnebusch adds, "loyalty to the individual states is contested by substate and suprastate identities. The resultant embedding of the state system is a matrix of fluid multiple identities".[26] And so, "built-in" anomalies of irredentist tendencies are characteristic of the region. They are reflected in the expression of the practices and worldviews of various ethnic and religious milieus, which challenge the immutability of territorial borders, thus simulating territorial conflict between states. Added to this is the immense and complicated power that political Islam possesses as a transnational, suprastate identity, which structures and commands the lives and worldviews of the people in the region. This makes the resort to the juncture of political identity and state sovereignty legitimate and wanting. Thus, the generated duality, which the ruling elite have to grapple with between asserting raison de la nation (pan-Arabism/pan-Islamism) and raison d'état (state sovereignty), is what has compelled them to treat the region as an arena of trans-state political competition.[27] How do democratisation theories grapple with the above notions, in light of the Arab Uprisings?

Democratization Theories: Contextual Literature Review

Three main theories might account for or explain the transition from autocracy to democratic rule in the setting of the third world model of the 'Arab Spring' or Arab Uprisings.[28]

First, Barrington Moore in his renowned book entitled *Social Origins of Dictatorship and Democracy*[29] argues, along Aristotelian lines (that the middle class acts as a buffer zone between the antagonism of the rich and poor), that the existence of a middle class is an essential ingredient or a guarantee to democracy. Moore calls for a balance of power between the middle class, on the one hand, and other classes, which might place impediments along the road of democracy, on the other. Moore stresses that the inculcation of the culture of democracy is contingent upon the ability of the middle class to disseminate its cultural, intellectual, and political influence, from the stance of its leading position in the economy and knowledge production.[30]

Second, Theda Skocpol in her two books entitled *States and Social Revolutions* and *Social Revolutions in the Third World*[31] added a new dimension to the middle class theory by including the concept of strong state and weak state. According to her, the strong state, allows the middle class to lead a smooth transition to democracy, while the weak state, stalls and obstructs that transition.[32]

Third, the Marxian-Weberian approach/tradition explains the saliency of capitalism as an embodiment of what Marx calls 'historical dialectical materialism'[33], and what Weber dubs as 'the age of modernity'. In this era, the industrial project resulted in a radical modification in the world of revolution, whereby society was preoccupied with other things than the previously dominant political arena. First, urbanisation took place whereby production moved from the village (rural) to the city (urban). Second, the vortex of the economy shifted from the landed elite to the business class entrepreneurs, which in turn resulted in the creation of crowded cities, which, in turn, gave way to new social classes. Religious myth were replaced by natural science and a new monopoly of knowledge that preaches inalienable rights instead of 'blue' or noble blood; the rule of law; and constitutionalism, or constitutional monarchies, in keeping with the motto of the French Revolution of 1789: liberty, fraternity, and equality.

If we take these three models as an ideal theoretical model for comparison, we will come to the conclusion of the structural impossibility of employing them as comparative-analytical frameworks in order to explain the phenomenon of the 'Arab Spring'. In spite of their growing numbers, the middle class is mostly composed of government or state employees in the countries experiencing the 'Arab Uprisings', the state being the largest employer. This means that those employees depend on the selling of their 'knowledge' in return for a salary i.e. most of them do not own productive sectors or have capital or own estates (cf. rentierism[34]). The middle class owes its social mobilization to the patronage/clientelism of an authoritarian state, and thus the middle class lacks the basic ingredients for democracy (or the 'democratic instinct') that characterised the middle class in the West, even in developing countries such as India. As Skocpol explained above, the Arab states are 'strong states', which derive their legitimacy from old/traditional tribal custom and laws, religion, traditional institutions, and ahistorical discourse, all of which existed before the modern state, and contest the authority of the state, endeavouring to establish an alternative sovereignty. These Arab states are mostly rentier states, which have monopoly over the natural resources and wealth, especially oil, and the sources of production, which are controlled by the power elite. Even in non-rentier states such as Lebanon, 2% of the population (the power elite) control 80% of the means of production and distribution. Thus, in the Arab countries experiencing the uprisings, the power elite control the junctures of the state, producing crony capitalism (Iraq, Syria, Egypt) and decapitated modernity, instead of a healthy democratic practice. Does the problem lie in the political systems, or with the tribal, patriarchal, and patrimonial way of governing?

A study of Arab political systems in the 20th century (which Juan Linz calls Sultanistic states[35] and Max Weber dubs Patrimonial states[36]) reveals that those systems have undergone political, social, and cultural transformations. The pressures on the system led to a degree of political-economic liberal openness as opposed to the earlier hegemony. Sultanistic states such as Bahrain, Yemen, and Morocco (Bahrain shifted from absolute monarch towards constitutional monarchy); previous totalitarian or authoritarian states (such as Egypt, Tunisia, and Iraq after the 2003 US-led invasion). All of these countries have undergone partial reform, or maybe the 'partial loosening of autocracy' might be a better term. Social protest movements originated in the latter (Tunisia, Egypt, Yemen), and soon spread to Sultanic states such as Oman and Saudi Arabia where the revolutions were crushed in their cradle, either by intimidation or the economic/moral incentive. For instance, in an attempt to quell social unrest, every Saudi citizen received a $38,000 state donation by way of material incentive to stay loyal. In addition to this, the Saudi government resorted to the religious-moral argument along the following lines: "Why are you rebelling? Others are rebelling in order to install an Islamic state, but you live in an Islamic state. Thus, dissent is unacceptable and will be hardly punished". Similarly, in Oman state repression reigned in the protesters. Although a few people were shot and killed in Oman, the state managed to co-opt the rest by way of the financial intensive and intimidation.

As mentioned in the introduction, in general, the Arab Spring constitutes a movement towards democratisation in its essence and orientation, but it lacks many credentials and ingredients of Western theories of democracy and societal transformation.

Factors Conducive to Social Change: Societal Transformation

Social change is contingent upon several variables or indicators: loss of legitimacy; deteriorating economy and brain drain; nationalism and the role of the state; the role of social media; lack of sovereignty; and the role of the military.

All Arab countries, irrespective of their political system, are plagued with loss, deterioration, or corrosion of legitimacy, especially among the youth who comprise around 70% of the population vis-à-vis the aging population , including the elite and the leaders of organized movements (such as the Muslim Brotherhood in Egypt and *al-Nahda*/Renaissance Party in Tunisia). Historic leaders relied on traditional charisma (tribal elderly); religious charisma (Imam Khumayni); revolutionary-popular charisma (Abd al-Nasser of Egypt); or artificial charisma (Saddam Husayn of Iraq). Historic examples of charismatic authority abound, but they are filled with slander and forgery such as President Sadat who was dubbed as the "hero of the passage (to Sinai)" or the "religious president". According to Max Weber, Charismatic authority is like an artificial creature that does not last for long since it becomes routinised and indigenous; as such, it is a threat to institutionalism and the rule of law. Thus, charismatic authority has to be replaced by the legal-rational authority in order to solve the structural problems rupturing society and in order to build a viable state. On the practical level, these autocratic regimes have lost their legitimacy: domestically because of state repression and holding to power in spite of the overwhelming will of the people for change; and internationally because the world community has declared these regimes as non-representative of their people, thus illegitimate.

The deteriorating economy, high-level of unemployment, meagre salaries, and brain drain are chronic ailments most Arab states face. Corruption is to the bone; dictators justify it by saying that corruption is the result of ordinary men having extraordinary temptations. Transparency and accountability are also lacking. The power elite steal with immunity and impunity. The billions of dollars – which autocratic leaders such as Mubarak of Egypt, Zayn al-'Abidin of Tunisia, and Qaddhafi of Libya – embezzled and appropriated from State treasury are indicative of the level of corruption rupturing these traditional societies. The solution seems easy, but is difficult to be implemented: the power elite should be barred from political office since they further their own interest and advantage to that of the state. Holding office and assigning political appointment should be based on meritocracy, rather than nepotism, favouritism, and in Lebanon's case, favouritism and sectarianism.

Concerning nationalism and the role of the state, the persons who spearheaded the social protest movement of the Arab Uprisings did not have a clear ideological agenda in mind, although there were politically driven groups such as the Islamists, nationalists, socialists, and liberals. The social network generation embraced neither the pre-World War II (WWII) multi-polarism nor the old Cold War bi-polarity (1945-1990), although they have post-colonial leanings. Therefore, the only venue left to unite these masses was nationalism. The discourse of the power elite in these countries was dated and failed to convince the mobilised masses since it was based on the 'imagined community' of the 'axis of resistance and confrontation' against the Israeli threat, imagined foreign threat (Syria), or real foreign threat (Bahrain). Those authoritarian, one-sided, futile discourses could not obscure the democratic discourse of the opposition. The most important dynamic of the Arab social protest movement might be the shift from confrontation with the other to the new psychology of self-reflection and evaluation in order to reform the self and society, at large.

Asef Bayat highlights the difficulty of planning a successful, yet peaceful uprising in an authoritarian state. Even when all the social conditions are met, it remains a challenging, complex, and daunting task to initiate revolutions. He attributes this to the 'highly complex nature of structural, international, coincidental and psychological factors'.[37] According to Bayat, revolutions result in a feeling of uneasiness and insecurity about the future, in terms of personal safety, the sustainability of the movement, and the successful transition to a more democratic polity. Many people exhibit the free rider's attitude, wanting others to carry out the revolution on their behalf. On these grounds, the youth of this social network revolution, of this Arab Spring, rebuked the average passive Arab citizens for not taking a firm stand with them against injustice and repression, calling them accomplices in the crimes the autocratic regimes are committing. This tone motivated undecided people to take a stance, to make their subaltern voices heard, rather than remaining on the margin, as they usually did. After all, a successful social or political protest has to do with the power and ability to muster an efficient mobilisation and the resilience to maintain it.

In this network and digital revolution age, other factors that are at play are the role of social media and the lack of state monopoly over production and consumption of information.[38] While in Egypt *Twitter* played a prominent role in mobilising the demonstrators and outsmarting the security forces, in Syria uploading videos on *Youtube* via satellite technology showed the world the other side of the coin, which state media was trying to hide. This is coupled by a lack of sovereignty. On the domestic level, these autocratic regimes are unrepresentative of people's sovereignty; on the regional and international levels, almost all Arab countries experiencing the Arab Uprisings are penetrated by state and non-state actors. Thus, applying Jean Bodin's definition of sovereignty as 'absolute, perpetual, and indivisible', all countries experiencing the Arab Spring appear to have lost their sovereignty, in one way or another.[39]

The seminal role of the military establishment and security apparatus ought not to be underestimated. It is most likely that the success or failure of social protest movements depends on the nature and structure of the military establishment as well as its stance towards the ongoing struggle between the ruling/power elite and the revolting masses. The military establishment is one of the state institutions mostly influenced by the elite, be it charismatic, institutional-legal (constitutional monarchies), absolute monarchies, or Patrimonial/ Sultanistic. Some state armies are semi-familial (Syria, Iraq, Libya, Yemen) as opposed to vocational in other countries such as (Egypt and Tunisia). From here originates the main difference regarding the stance from social protest movements and the role and behaviour of the military institution and security apparatus: either to support, or be neutral, or even to disintegrate. This has to do mainly with the military's initial role and contribution to state building. Indeed, this historic connection between the military establishment and the founding of the state ought not to be underestimated since the more these are juxtaposed, the stronger and smoother is the transition and vice versa (mainly due to the dissemination of networks of patrimonial, tribal/sectarian, or party allegiance). It is most likely that civil or social protest movements have more potential to change the status quo in countries where the military establishment played a structural role in the founding of the state (Tunisia) in contrast to the military's charismatic, hegemonic role in the state of transition (Egypt).

Do the aforementioned exposition of theories and their applications posit the structural impossibility between the Arab Spring and democratisation and liberalisation processes? Are these theories untenable?

Theoretical Conclusions and Practical Applications

After the end of the Cold War around 1990, the international community placed heavy emphasis on political reform and economic openness as new elements in foreign policy, which aim at creating a global environment based upon free market economy and political democracy, without giving away traditional foreign policy constituents such as strategic balances and economic interests. This duel policy is conducive to the development of social protest movements as well as the status and interest of the states that follow such policies. However, there are countries swimming against the current such as Russia, China, and Iran. After 9/11, the international community doubled its pressure by imposing reform agendas on states in an attempt to 'dry out the sources of terror'. Evidently, this led to loopholes and drawbacks since most of the targeted countries were strong states. Concerning social protest movements in the Middle East, we notice that the international community intervened through different means: political pressure in order to initiate reform (Egypt); direct foreign intervention in order to impose regime change (Libya: UNSC Resolution 1973: No fly zone and protecting civilians); diplomacy, negotiations, bargaining and political pressure in order to promote/impose a solution or forge an agreement (Yemen); and a little bit of both (Syria and Bahrain)

Implications of a new understanding of the democratic transformation processes

The Arabs are still looking for their homegrown version of democracy. Even in the West, democracy is not the abode of reconciliation and harmony; rather, it is an open public space, a public sphere where opposing views and opinions battle with word and action. The rudimentary forms of the nascent Arab democratization and liberalization processes, which are contesting the Arab public sphere, have created a 'democracy without democrats'.[40] It seems that political theoreticians in the West subscribe to the following formula: free market economy is conducive or leads to democracy. However, Egyptian economic openness produced an alliance between the business class and the political elite, which made it a democracy without freedoms.

Democracy has obvious structural foundations. First, it is based on the separation of powers between the executive, legislative, and judicial branches and the checks and balances among them. These foundational, normative bases are either still lacking or have embryonic or rudimentary foundations in most Arab countries. Tunisia seems to fair better than other Arab countries undergoing the liberalization process. In Egypt, Libya, and Yemen it remains a rocky process. Second is the dichotomy between the produce of the revolution and the state; or, in other words, the separation between civil society and political society. Concentration of the two leads to a destructive monopoly of the concept and practice of freedom. Market economy is still weak, by all standards. One main reason is that the middle class exclusively relies on wages, rather than ownership although it is the most dominant social class in urban societies. Nevertheless, its potential is still curtailed, with the possibility of a few exceptions. Third, democracy depends on the rule of law. Unfortunately, in third world societies, tradition and tribalism (tribal customs) are stronger than law. Also, the notion that the ruler is above the law is still dominant, i.e. he alone has the prerogative to interpret the law and pretend that he is the spokesman on behalf of Islamic law (*Shari'a*). Fourth, democracy needs an international milieu, an environment that is capable of providing a supporter to it, fending for it, and protecting it. However, our world is still dominated by tyrants, those who pretend to be holy or wear revolutionary garments. The separation of powers and checks and balances are the bases of democracy, where monopoly and concentration of power are prohibited. Political parties that came to power by the ballot do not have a de facto legitimacy as a military leader who came by a military coup (which is the case in most Arab countries). In these societies, the perpetuation of legitimacy depends on solving the current problems, primarily the staggering economy. After all, people do not live on ideology alone; they need bread and butter.

In the Middle East or the countries experiencing the Arab Uprisings, democratisation and liberalisation processes – especially the transition to democracy – are still in their evolutionary stage. The power elite could monopolise or obstruct these processes in the face of massive popular support for change. One hopes that the dynamic momentum of the democratisation and liberalisation processes will gain foothold and find currency in countries like Iran, China, and Russia, although in social science repercussions, ripple effects, or even regressions cannot be ruled out. 'Theocratic' Saudi Arabia and 'hierocratic' Iran with their authoritarian-religious regimes pose an impediment to democratic development, an obstacle that would not be removed except by reforming both systems. As such, their selective support of social protest movements is contingent upon state interest or their ideological leanings. The Gulf Cooperation Council (GCC), mostly Saudi and Qatar, are pumping money to the Islamists in order to create an environment that supports their traditional political systems. Iran sees in the coming of Islamists to power the advent of strong powers that oppose the US hegemony and its agenda in the Middle East. Change in Iran seems to be on the way, but it might take a long time to materialise. Noteworthy, 82% of the population are youth who were born after the 1979 Revolution. Those predominantly want better relations with the US and the West. The nuclear deal signed on 24 November 2013 could be seen as a first step in this direction.[41]

Hizbullah's Post-Islamist Trend?

Arguing along the lines of Olivier Roy,[42] Farhad Khosrokhavar,[43] Gille Kepel,[44] Peter Mandaville,[45] Amel Boubekeur,[46] Asef Bayat,[47] and others, I would like to point to a general tendency of a gradual transition from Islamism to post-Islamism, from the 'old' to the 'new.'[48] Asef Bayat had a pioneering contribution to the term 'post-Islamism' as early as 1996 and distinguished himself from other scholars,[49] who employed the concept, but apparently with different connotations. According to Bayat, post-Islamism represents in the first place a *condition*, a social and political one, in which the appeal and the sources for legitimacy of Islamist politics get exhausted after a phase of experimentation. The adherents become aware of the anomalies and shortcomings of their system while attempting to moderate and institutionalize their movement.[50] Post-Islamism is also a *project* representing a conscious attempt to transcend Islamism in social, political, and intellectual domains. Thus, it is an endeavour in overturning the underlying singular authoritative voice of Islamism and replacing it with a plurality of voices of authority, i.e. 'emphasizing rights instead of duties; historicity rather than fixed Holy Scriptures; freedom instead of rigidity; and the future instead of the past'. Yet, it is neither anti-Islamic nor un-Islamic or secular; rather, it is an undertaking to fuse 'religiosity and rights, Islam and liberty, faith and freedom'. The Islamic social movement's ideology becomes plural in this state, not basing itself solely on Islam, but becoming capable of including other (secular) ideas and denominations.[51]

My interviewees from Hizbullah's rank and file defined 'Islamists' as fervent Muslim believers or pious (religious) youth, and 'Islamism' as religiosity and strict adherence to the divine laws. They defined post-Islamism as a process of *infitah*, or opening-up to global cultural trends while preserving indigenous values as an Islamic moral alternative.[52] How post-Islamist, then, Hizbullah has become, if at all? Is Hizbullah on a trajectory of post-Islamism, or is its *infitah* to be understood as Mandaville characterized as bottom-up Islamization in disguise?[53]

Antonio Gramsci argued, "All the essential questions of sociology are nothing than questions of political science".[54] Paraphrasing Gramsci, social movements are nothing but political movements. However, "modern social movements are primarily social and not directly political in character. Their aim is the mobilization of civil society, not the seizure of power".[55] Relying on Gramsci's interplay between the social and political, as well as Bayat's bifurcation of political Islam into 'Islamism' and 'post-Islamism', I nuance Bayat's definition along these lines: (1) Islamism has to do with a top-down hegemony aimed at destroying the political system, killing the power/ruling elite, and establishing an Islamic order in its place where Islamic Law (*Shari'a*) reigns. Examples are al-Qa'ida and its offshoots, the Taliban in Pakistan and Afghanistan, and *takfiri* groups. Islamic groups that portray a post-Islamist trend aim at a bottom-up integration in the political system, state institutions, and the overall public sphere through diplomacy, negotiations, compromises, and bargaining, as *al-Nahda* in Tunisia (2011 to the present), the Muslim Brotherhood in Egypt (2010-12), Hamas in the Occupied Territories (winning the 2006 elections after 40 years hegemony of the PLO), and Hizbullah after 1992, etc. In this chapter, I limit myself to the Lebanese Hizbullah.

As Asef Bayat argued, the line between Islamism and post-Islamism is sometimes difficult to delineate, or an Islamic movement can be Islamist at a certain stage of its development, and later on, it may start to convey post-Islamist trends and trajectories such as Hizbullah.

Hizbullah witnessed remarkable transformations in the past three decades. From its founding as an Islamist movement of social and political protest anathematising the political order and regarding the Lebanese state as an apostate in the 1980s, to a parliamentary political party since 1992. Hizbullah's metamorphosis could be attributed to changed historical and social circumstances and, more importantly (using Alexander Wendt's insights above), to the results of interactions with other political actors. Thus, the objective, sociological, and political reality of Lebanon compelled this originally Islamist movement onto the post-Islamist path, even though such post-Islamism remains inconsistent, selective, and pragmatic. It seems Hizbullah is still experimenting with the tenets of post-Islamism.

The Lebanese Hizbullah as a Case Study

"The emergence of socio-religious movements [e.g. Hizbullah] are important to examine, especially in the ways that they challenge and/or intersect with nation-state projects on identity, justice, welfare and secular modernist notions of body, self and gender."[56]

As mentioned above, in his notion of social construction, Alexander Wendt argued that social identities are 'identities that political actors generate through interaction with other actors'.[57] Applying this reading to Hizbullah, one could argue that the party changed due to historical and social circumstances as well as interactions with other political actors. This constitutes the kernel and fulcrum of Hizbullah's *infitah* ('opening-up') policy. Further measures of political compromise such as conceding ministerial quotas to Sunni and Christian representatives in the cabinet suggest that Hizbullah remains committed indeed to a mode of governance that is inherently communal, pluralist, and representative. Domestically, the interplay between identity and state sovereignty are visibly at play. For example, post-2005 policy statements of the Lebanese governments contained a security statement, which continued to balance the dynamic between Hizbullah's resistance identity and the Lebanese state's sovereignty. For instance, article six of the Lebanese Government's 2009 Policy Statement read: "From the stance of the duty to uphold Lebanese sovereignty and territorial integrity, the cabinet affirms the right of Lebanon, its government, its people, its army, and its Resistance [Hizbullah] to employ all legitimate means in order to liberate all Lebanese territory."[58]

Hizbullah's *Infitah* Policy and the Arab Spring

In his latest publications on the Arab Spring, Olivier Roy's thesis is that the Islamists did not change; rather, they altered their strategies and policies, and maybe modified their vision, in order to adapt to the wind of change resulting from the popular uprisings.[59] How does Hizbullah's *infitah* policy comport with the tenets of the Arab Spring? Interpreting this along the lines of rational choice theory, MP 'Ali Fayyad[60] told me, "what we witness now in the Arab World is the reconciliation of the

Islamic vision [Hizbullah's vision] with the necessity of communication, *infitah*, moderation, and reality" (*realpolitik*), which ties in nicely with Alexander Wendt's theory above. Fayyad adds, "the Islamists became less ideological and more political. Their views on power, authority, and governing shifted from crude ideology towards an intellectual-practical thinking, which is more open to the overall social and national interest."

Employing the contextual approach, Hajj Muhammad Ra'd – the head of the party's parliamentary bloc and member of the Consultative (*Shura*) Council – told me that the 'Buazizi Syndrome'[61] will lead to different results in different countries. In other words, the democratisation and liberalisation process ignited by the Arab Spring is of an uncertain future, taking into consideration the resilience of the Arab autocratic regimes.[62] Hajj Ghalib Abu Zaynab, Hizbullah's officer for Christian-Muslim Understanding, affirmed that if the Arab Spring leads to institutionalism and the rule of law, then the Islamists' call for freedom, dignity, and social justice would be realized in part.[63]

In turn, MP 'Ali Fayyad attributes this line of thinking to the insights and impact of Habermas's theory of communicative action on the Arab and Islamic world. Moreover, Fayyad also subscribes to Roy's theory. He interprets Hizbullah's *infitah* along these lines, in the sense that the party had to 'reinvent' itself by basing itself on Sayyid 'Abbas's vision of *infitah*. From this perspective, according to Fayyad, Hizbullah's 'Arab Spring' began in the early 1990s through its policy of *infitah*.[64] *Infitah* started on a small scale when Hizbullah began to voice the grievances of the Lebanese subaltern classes, irrespective if they were Muslims or Christian-- irrespective if they were Sunnis, Druz, or Shi'ites. This amounts to a complete overhaul in Hizbullah's political strategy in the 1980s, which mainly targeted its Shi'ite constituency, to the exception of others.

My reading of Hizbullah's rise to political power in Lebanon is that, the political reinvention of the movement is intricately related to the expansion of the social constituency it addresses. Accordingly, the Arab Spring seems to be part of a larger social churning in the Arab world, of which Hizbullah's rise to political power was yet another manifestation.

The Advent of the Arab Spring: A 'Social Network' Revolution?

Many theories tried to explain the phenomenon of the Arab Uprisings. In addition to Habermas's theory of communicative action and the public sphere, Anderson, Eickelman, Bunt, Scott and Carrington, Castells, etc. subscribe to the social network theory, terming the Arab uprisings as social network revolutions, or at least arguing that this quest of freedom, dignity, and democracy was fuelled and organized, in part, by the social networks and digital activism.[65] From this perspective, Lynch adds

> So while the Arab uprisings generated a marvelous range of innovative tactics (uploading mobile-camera videos to social media like Facebook and Twitter, seizing and holding public squares), they did not introduce any particularly new ideas[66]... It pioneered the use of social media, mastered the art of symbolic demonstrations, and pried open a space in the [...] media... The relentless critique of the status quo, the generational desire for political change, the yearning for democratic freedoms, the intense pan-Arab identification – these had all been in circulation for more than a decade. What changed with the fall of ... [the autocratic Arab regimes in Tunisia, Egypt, Libya, and Yemen] ... was the recognition that even the worst tyrants could be toppled. It shattered the wall of fear.[67]

In the age of globalization, 'shattering the wall of fear' implies that there is a dialectical relationship between the internal and external, between the domestic and foreign. Despotic regimes cannot anymore have a monopoly over the dissemination and consumption of information. They cannot brainwash and indoctrinate their citizens as subjects. Thanks to the social network revolution, this network society whipped tyranny with innovation, thus it was able to shatter the myth of a 'closed society' in its struggle, drive, and aspiration towards realizing an open, democratic society.

One way of examining the intricate social dynamics that motivated Hizbullah's *infitah*, is to study the way in which individuals, groups, movements, in particular, the youth affect the contours of social and political change in today's Arab world. Are social/Islamic movements capable of leading a peaceful democratic transition in the Arab world? While the 1989 revolutions in Eastern Europe led to an almost complete change in terms of political and economic systems, in the Arab world, one has to keep in mind the resilience of social, political, and economic "structures" in offsetting these new social movements' desire for change. As radical and groundbreaking the Arab revolutions may appear to be after decades of authoritarian rule, will they lead to a complete overhaul in the system, or will they fall short of these expectations? Will they be reduced to 'refolutions'[68] and recycle and perpetuate the existing regimes and the ruling elite? Will they end up piecing together existing socio-political structures in their attempt to reform what is already there, as exemplified by Tunisia and Egypt? It is interesting to observe how the populace are going to uproot these illegitimate, corrupt-tyrannical regimes in their struggle to override despotism, with constitutionalism and institutionalism.

We are yet to see how this new social movement is going to empower the people of the region and the Arab and Muslim world in general. It is interesting to note that Asef Bayat anticipated many of these sweeping changes before the Arab Spring was launched. As the title of his book suggests, Bayat believed that ordinary people can change the Middle East, and they did.[69] However, he admonished that it is a 'long revolution', "a process which is 'difficult', in the sense of complex and multifaceted, 'total', meaning not just economic but social and cultural transformation, and 'human', involving the deepest structures of relations and feelings".[70]

Hizbullah's Stance on the Arab Spring

Hizbullah was elated by the Tunisian and Egyptian street politics and youth power. In this Arab Spring, Hizbullah issued political declarations blessing the Tunisian and Egyptian people, in particular, and the Arab masses, in general, for their drive for "freedom and dignity." Hizbullah's Secretary General Sayyid Hasan Nasrallah added, "This is the true path when people believe in their resolve… this is the new Middle East created by its own people." He concluded, "Your Spring has begun; no one can lead you to another winter. Your belief, vigilance, and resilience will overcome all difficulties and make you triumphant".[71]

Hizbullah supported the Arab street with the exception of Syria, where it adamantly stood by the Syrian regime, its indispensable strategic ally. Hizbullah lent its coreligionist Bahraini populace unwavering support in the face of the Sunni ruling elite. This stance led some political analysts to criticize such 'double standards'. Being on the defensive, Nasrallah tried to defend, justify, and legitimize Hizbullah's policies. In terms of geopolitics, Hizbullah has repeatedly stated that it would not interfere in any military attack targeting Syria and Iran, unless there is an existential danger facing the two regimes, whereby Hizbullah's joining the fight would tilt the balance in favour of the aggressed upon parties.

A Cry for Freedom: 'People want the Downfall of the Regime'

In less than a month, two Arab leaders were deposed by the people's power. Are the 1989 winds of change blowing across the Arab world? As the Middle East and North Africa (MENA) region is engulfed with protests portraying the affirmation of the will of the people after decades of authoritarian rule, Lebanon does not remain the anomaly; rather change has been instigated by an unexpected actor. The catalyst was Tunisia's Jasmine uprising[72] that ended the 23-year old rule of president bin 'Ali after the army supported the uprising and ousted him into exile in Saudi Arabia on 14 January 2011. This paved the way for the return, on 30 January 2011, of the moderate Islamist intellectual Rashid al-Ghannushi, the leader of the 'Renaissance Movement' (*al-Nahda*) which he founded in 1981. He returned to his country after 22 years in exile in London, to participate in the parliamentary elections conducted on 23 October 2011. *Al-Nahda* won 41% of the seats, thus becoming the largest political party in Tunisia.

From 25 January to 11 February 2011[73], after eighteen days of massive demonstrations that claimed the lives of more than 350 people throughout Egypt, the most populous Arab country with the largest army in the Middle East, the social-network revolution succeeded in ousting president Mubarak after 30 years of autocratic rule. After three days, on 14

February, the military establishment set itself in power for the coming six months, after dissolving the legislature and suspending the constitution. On 30 November, parliamentary elections took place, whereby the Islamists – the Muslim Brotherhood (MB) and *al-Nour* Salafist party – won almost 70% of the vote. On 15 June 2012, the military stretched its wings and flexed its muscles: it established the Supreme Council of the Armed Forces (SCAF). The SCAF consolidated its power by dissolving parliament and confiscating its legislating power. After 15 days, on 30 June, the first democratically elected and civilian president, Muhammad Morsi of the MB, was sworn in. July 2012 witnessed a tug of war between Morsi and SCAF, both of whom were vying to consolidate power. In a brilliant move, on 12 August 2012, Morsi offered early retirement to the defence minister and Army Chief of Staff Tantawi, the SCAF de facto ruler of the country. However, Morsi made the fatal mistake of issuing a presidential declaration that consolidated his power and confiscated the role of the legislature and the executive, and on 22 November, he issued another decree that sidelined the judiciary. On 29 November, the Islamists approved a draft constitution that granted them power, at the expense of the minorities, liberals, and socialists, the real initiators of the revolution. The economic and political situation continued to deteriorate in 2013. In June 2013, at least 17 million Egyptians took to the streets to vent their anger demanding the ousting of Morsi, ushering a second revolution. By the end of the month, the scene was of bloody confrontations that killed and wounded many demonstrators. On 3 July, the military heeded the calls of the street by stepping in to end the blood bath. General Sisi, the minister of defence, ousted Morsi, suspended the constitution, appointed a caretaker government, and arrested Morsi. The next day an interim president was sworn in, in conformity with the stipulations of the constitution in place. Alienating the Islamists, a new government was sworn in on 13 July 2013 without them. On 14 August, the security forces stormed the sit-ins of Morsi's supporters, killing and wounding hundreds. On 23 September 2013, the state judiciary banned the Muslim Brotherhood, but the party remained operation, both in public and underground.

As Nawal al-Saadawi told me, "We deposed two presidents: the first Mubarak, an autocrat who ruled for 30 years; the second, a 'democratically elected' Mursi who concentrated power, abided by the dictates of his 'spiritual leader', and failed to realize the dreams and aspiration of the Egyptian Revolution". When I asked her about the future of the Arab uprisings, she replied that she was cautiously optimistic: "I will not lose hope; hope gives strength, it is strength; hope is the building block of the future".[74]

Al-Saadawi wrote that the initiators of the uprisings, the 'true revolutionaries', never reap the glory. It is always other forces – the most organized and those who have a strong social base in the community – who reap the glory and come to prominence. In this context, the story of the Muslim Brotherhood in Egypt is telling. Sadaawi believes that all revolutions need time to unfold, such as the French revolution, which was moving at the pace of two steps forward, one step backward, but the process is straight ahead. The Arab Spring is passing through the same process. The Arab Uprisings are moving in a zigzag process, not a straight elevation. Sadaawi argues that the Arab Uprisings are of a political nature. She thinks that in order to have a strong impact on society, political revolutions should be accompanied by cultural, educational, and economic revolutions.[75]

While in Tunisia and Egypt street politics led to a regime change, its domino effect swept throughout the region with varying degrees of success. In Morocco, Algeria, Bahrain, Sudan, Jordan, Kuwait, Oman, Mauritania, Iraq, and Saudi Arabia demonstrations were more restrained and did not muster much following, thus failing to initiate regime change. These were subdued by the ruling/power elite, who offered marginal concessions. Even in Iran 'The Green Movement' was emboldened and empowered by the Arab Spring, when it staged demonstrations against the regime after hibernating for months.

In Libya, the '17th of February Revolution' deteriorated into protracted civil war that claimed the lives of thousands. Belatedly, on 17 March 2011, The United Nations Security Council (UNSC) Resolution 1973 imposed a no-fly zone that mainly aimed at protecting civilians. Two days later, operation 'Odyssey Dawn' was launched by France, Britain, the US, and other NATO countries in order to impose Resolution 1973 by military force. Libya was the third Muslim country the US attacks after Afghanistan and Iraq, but this time not in an anti-terrorism campaign, rather in support of the 'democratic movement'. The 42-year old regime of Colonel Qadhdhafi collapsed on 23 September 2011 after Tripoli fell to the revolutionaries. Subsequently, the rebels captured Qadhdhafi's hometown *Sirt* and executed him on 20 October 2011.[76] Hizbullah has a vested interest in the downfall of the 'oppressive' Libyan regime since it accusers it of 'concealing' the leader of the Shi'ite community in Lebanon, Imam Musa al-Sadr, during his official visit in August 1978.

Hizbullah was accused of siding with the dissident Shi'ite *Huthis* even before the outbreak of the Yemini revolution of 27 January 2011. After military confrontations, tribal struggles, and civil war symptoms, on 23 November 2011, the Gulf Cooperation Council (GCC), operating under the banner of the Arab League, succeeded in brokering a deal whereby president 'Ali Abdallah Saleh promised to relinquish power to his deputy Abd Rabu Mansur al-Hadi. However, this move came into effect on 21 January 2012, after Saleh received immunity from persecution from the Yemini parliament. Although Yemen still faces challenges from the transnational *al-Qa'ida* organization and other local dissident groups, which were operational before the enunciation of the Arab Spring, hopefully the Yemini chapter was put to close after 99.8% of the 6.6 million Yemini voters gave their confidence in a national referendum to al-Hadi, the first president from South Yemen, on 21 February 2012.[77]

In Bahrain, the ongoing '14 of February' revolution has been violently suppressed by the regime. Hizbullah is very vocal against the regime that is suppressing the Bahrainis from 'revealing the injustices' (*izhar al-mazlumiyya*) they are suffering from, and Nasrallah has compared the Al Khalifa ruling family to Mubarak and Qadhdhafi.[78]

In Syria, Hizbullah's strategic ally, repeated Russian and Chinese veto at the UNSC prevented the international community's intervention to enforce a regime change, as was the case in Libya, even after two years of its flare up on 15 March 2011. Although a referendum on a new pluralistic constitution[79] took place on 26 February 2012, the Syrian civil war still raged on. Initially, the six-point plan of Kofi Annan – the Joint Special Envoy of the UN and the Arab League – appeared to have partially quelled the violence. Annan succeeded to broker a nominal sensation of hostilities on 12 April at 3:00 GMT. Two days later, on 14 April, in an unprecedented move, the UNSC unanimously adopted Resolution 2024, which called for dispatching 30 unarmed international observers to monitor the cease-fire.[80] On 19 April 2012, Syria signed with the UN the protocol delineating the work of the observers. It seemed that the Syrian crisis was veering towards a political solution, rather than a military one, as Nasrallah predicted in his 17 April 2013 interview. Nasrallah affirmed that he is 'a friend of Syria, but he is not a Syrian agent'.[81]

Nevertheless, a political solution remained a distant dream, even after Lakhdar Brahimi replaced Annan. The Syrian crisis degenerated into a protracted civil war: state repression continued, and the Free Syrian Army (FSA) resumed its fight to oust the regime, emboldened by the joining the fight on its side of hard-core al-Qa'ida affiliated Islamists and foreign jihadis. Initially, this gave the FSA a moral boost and a front lead over the regular Syrian Army, but not for long. Internal fighting erupted between the Islamists and the FSA, which eventually weakened both and led the regime forces to take the initiate and regain strategic terrain, and thus prolonged the civil war, after many political analysts predicted the fall of the Syrian regime in a few months. In my interview with *France 24* on 29 November 2013, I made a heuristic comparison, an analogy between the Lebanese civil war and the Syrian civil war, forecasting a long and bitter conflict in Syria.[82]

Like the Lebanese war became the 'war of others on Lebanese soil', the Syrian conflict degenerated into a regional war, whereby Saudi Arabia, Qatar, and Turkey were supporting the opposition militarily and logistically, while Iran, Iraq, and Hizbullah were supporting the regime in a similar fashion. International players also weighed in, whereby France, UK, and the US supported the opposition, while Russia and China buttressed the regime.

Breaching Regional Sovereignty: Hizbullah's Involvement in the Syrian Quagmire and the Lebanese Repercussions

On 25 May 2013, Nasrallah deemed it an existential necessity and blatantly announced that Hizbullah has entered the Syrian fight on the side of the regime. Invoking the 'Divine Victory' legacy of 2006 July War with Israel, Nasrallah emphatically promised his constituency another victory, which materialized on 12 June 2013, when the party 'liberated' *Qusayr* from the Syrian opposition fighters.[83]

Alagha states that the Party's Secretary General, Sayyid Nasrallah, declared only to resort to fighting in Syria in case of extreme necessity. The fact that the Hezbollah has publicly acknowledged its involvement in Syria ought to raise alarm bells for all "experts" across/on the region. Given that Alagha's book demonstrates how politically astute and capable the Hezbollah political leadership has been over the years, for Sayyid Nasrallah to make the extreme decision to be involved in Syria, a decision that he knows will probably be fatal to its party's stand on the Lebanese political scene, ought not to be dismissed as just a political mistake, but as a suicide mission, a last cartridge to counter what is certainly perceived as a deadly force against Shi'a Islam's survival in the region. Perception here is a word of great importance, because as Alagha states, while a phobia of Sunni Islam may well be over-rated, the reality that it generates is what will have to be dealt with in the region's immediate future, a seed planted more than ten years ago in newly-"liberated" Iraq. Once again, blinded by their own racism, most Hezbollah "experts" have retreated to their comfort zone in misunderstanding the urgency of Nasrallah's perception surrounding Syria, privileging a narrative of Arab impulsiveness and inherent political senselessness over one of survival.[84]

Employing anti-*takfiri* discourse, Hizbullah interfered in the sovereignty and territorial integrity of Syria in order to protect its back and fend off the militant Sunni fundamentalist threat originating from there. Of course, Hizbullah's military involvement was welcomed by its strategic ally, the Syrian regime, which considers it a boost in its fight against 'armed gangs' (SLA) and 'international terrorism' or 'jihadis affiliated with al-Qa'ida', as the Syrian regime labels the military opposition. Hizbullah accused the FAS as being traitors, collaborators with the 'enemy', as the defunct South Lebanon Army (SLA) did during the IDF occupation of southern Lebanon. As such, Hizbullah accused the SLA of furthering the Israeli-US agenda in the Middle East, or of creating the 'New Middle East of Condoleeza Rice', the ex-Secretary of State.

Domestically, Hizbullah traded accusations with the Western-backed March 14 coalition, which compared Hizbullah's military intervention in Syria with the Israeli Defence Forces (IDF) occupation of Lebanon in order to protect Israel from the attacks of the Lebanese and Palestinian resistance. According to March 14, Hizbullah behaved like the IDF by invading and occupying land and encroaching on the 'sovereignty and territorial integrity' of Syria, a UN member country, in order to protect its back, élan vital. Furthermore, March 14 argued that Hizbullah's involvement in the Syrian civil war is diminishing its availability across the Lebanese-Israeli boarder and is distracting its vigilance in dealing with any Israeli imminent threat.

Due to its strategic interest and its fear of losing its backyard, its 'vital space' (élan vital), as well as an easy weapon's supply route, Hizbullah involved itself in the Syrian quagmire. It sent fighters, in spite of the heavy blood price it has to pay and the fear of depleting its human and material resources, especially after losing fighters everyday. Sayyid Nasrallah conceded Hizbullah's limited capabilities and argued that his party cannot change the outcome of the Syrian war, but can offer logistical and material help to the Syrian Army and train it for guerrilla warfare: 'We went to Syria to defend Lebanon… we did it by a personal decision, rather than heeding an Iranian order'. Nasrallah accused Saudi Arabia of waging proxy wars in Iran, Iraq, Lebanon, and more importantly in Syria by its material and military support of radical Islamist groups fighting the regime.[85]

In addition to many radical Lebanese Sunni Islamists volunteering to fight against the Syrian regime, jihadi Salafis such as the Shaykh Ahmad al-Asir of Sidon and Shaykh Salem al-Rāfi'i of Tripoli sent fighters en masse. The Sunni-Shi'a strife (*fitna*) in Lebanon appeared to be unavoidable. On 23 June 2013, violent military clashes in Sidon erupted between Hizbullah and Shaykh Ahmad al-Asir supporters. After many dead and wounded fell, the Lebanese Army intervened and ended the fight, but at a high price. Al-Asir's headquarters were destroyed and many of his supporters were arrested. Al-Asir fled and his whereabouts are unknown to date. My omen became a painful reality when, on 19 November 2013, two supporters of al-Asir conducted a twin-suicide operation against the Iranian Embassy, located at *Dahiya* – the heart of Hizbullah's den and stronghold of the southern suburb of Beirut, killing 23 people. Previously, the *Dahiya* was targeted by rockets and two massive explosions: the first on 7 July 2013 led to a few deaths, while that of 15 August 2013, killed 31 people, after which Hizbullah agreed to the deployment of the Lebanese Army and security forces. On 16 January 2014, a suicide bomber detonated a car in *Hirmel*, Hizbullah's stronghold in the *Biqa'*, killing three and wounding more than 46. For the next two days, the Syrian Islamists continued to target *Hirmel* with sporadic rockets.

On 28 September 2013, violent confrontations erupted between militant Sunnis and Hizbullah fighters in the *Balbaak*, on the Eastern *Biqa'* valley. As was the case in *Dahiya*, this eventually led to the deployment of the Lebanese Army and security forces in the city, thus returning sovereignty to the state after the apparent failure of private security measures for a second time. On 23 August 2013, two car bombs targeted two Sunni mosques in Tripoli, north Lebanon – the second largest Sunni city after Beirut. Regular skirmishes and seven mini-wars in Tripoli erupted between the Sunnis, who support March 14, and the 'Alawis, who support the Syrian regime. Unfortunately, what I admonished against two years ago when I wrote *Hizbullah's DNA and the Arab Spring* – namely that the Syrian uprising will spill over to Lebanon with drastic and detrimental consequences, the most salient of which is the feared Sunni-Shi'a discord (*fitna*) – became a painful reality in both countries.[86]

Domestically, the Syrian war led to the postponement of the legislative elections in Lebanon (for the first time since the end of the civil war in 1990), a political deadlock and stalemate, and an unprecedented political paralysis. Beside a caretaker government (cabinet) and a constitutionally weakened president, Lebanon was witnessing a power vacuum, the paralysis of institutions, and the hovering omen of civil unrest. Deferring the political situation in Lebanon to the fate of Syrian president, in a ten-minute session on 31 March 2013, the Lebanese parliament extended its mandate by 15 months to 20 November 2014, i.e. till after the scheduled Syrian presidential elections in June 2014. The cabinet resigned on 22 March 2013 after internal feuds made its proper functioning impossible. For the next eight months, there was no change in the situation. This is unprecedented in Lebanese history: in 1969, it took the late PM Rashid Karami 194 days to form the cabinet.[87] It seems that power vacuum in Lebanon serves Hizbullah's interests, although the discourse of its leading cadres is otherwise. Even if a government is solely formed by Hizbullah and its allies, such an institutional structure might curtail the party's freedom of movement due to diplomacy, negotiations, bargaining, and possible concessions, which characterise the Lebanese 'consociational'/consensual political system.

The Deals with Syria and Iran

The international and regional dynamics and the rules of the game changed when Syria signed a chemical weapon's deal with the UN, and Iran signed a nuclear agreement with the five permanent members of the UNSC and Russia. These breakthroughs seem to convey the new approach the international community is taking against the previously considered rogue states.

After the chemical attack of 21 August 2013 on a suburb of Damascus, which led to hundreds of civilian death and wounded, a US-Russian agreement brokered on 14 September 2013 opened the door for destruction of the Syrian chemical weapons stock piles. By the end of October 2013, the OPCW[88] dismantled and obliterated Syria's chemical weapons manufacturing and mixing equipment, as stipulated by UNSC Resolution 2118, which was adopted unanimously on 27 September

2011. Work remains on the way and in tandem to pacify and destroy all of Syria's chemical weapons.

After almost ten years of deadlock, Iran came clean on its nuclear program when it forged in Geneva, Switzerland a four-page agreement/deal with the International Community (P5+1)[89] on 24 November 2013.[90] The deal gave more transparency and accountability to the IAEA in conducting its inspection and monitoring of the Iranian nuclear facilities.

The deals between Syria and Iran and the international community changed the rules of the game, eased the pressure on two previously considered rogue nations (Iran was part of President Bush's part of the "axis of evil") and welcomed them to the world of nations after the US declared the Syrian regime as 'illegitimate' and the Iranian regime as a 'sponsor of terrorism'. This resulted in new dynamics whereby Syria was given a free hand in its use of conventional weapons to stamp out the military opposition. At least the international community seems to turn a blind eye and a deaf eye to the excessive use of force by the Syrian regime on the rebels, even if this led to massive civilian death, as the regime justifies these acts by recourse to the theory of collateral damage, arguing that 'armed gangs' are hiding behind civilians and using them as 'human shields'. Hizbullah's Secretary General Sayyid Hasan Nasrallah argued that after those deals, Syria and Iran will not exert pressure on Hizbullah to change its policies. On the contrary, he claimed that the agreements proved that American hegemony is on the wane and the international arena is governed by a multi-polar system where various actors are contesting this international space. Nasrallah contended that this new reality would have a positive impact on the party and will give it a freer hand in exercising its domestic and regional hegemony: "The winners from the Iranian deal are the people of the Middle East."[91]

Shattering Relations with the Palestinians

On the eve of the third anniversary of the Syrian revolution, on 16 March 2014, Hizbullah seems to be more isolated than ever, especially from Sunni mainstream actors. The majority of the Palestinian factions are against the Syrian regime: Hamas[92], the PLO, and the jihadi Salafis.

For instance, on 4 December 2012, the Palestinian Jihadi Salafi Ansar Allah[93] dissociated itself from Hizbullah and sent jihadis to fight the Syrian regime. Recurrent clashes between Hizbullah and Palestinian factions – such Hamas, the PLO, Popular Front for the Liberation of Palestine-General Command (PFLP-GC) and the Democratic Front for the Liberation of Palestine (DFLP) – are telling of the dire straits Hizbullah is facing in trying to maintain an alliance with the Sunnis.

Final Word

Is Hizbullah's commitment to the Arab Spring absolute and irrevocable, or is it circumstantial and selective based on serving its own narrow interest? Is Hizbullah blindly supporting the Shi'ites irrespective if they are rulers or ruled, 'oppressors' or 'oppressed'? Is it employing 'double standards', a charge it accuses its enemies of? Is there smoke without fire? Would Hizbullah's practices pertaining to the Arab Spring reduce its pan-Arab, pan-Islamic appeal? Hizbullah's support of the minority 'Shi'ite' 'Alawi Syrian regime against the majority of the Sunni population; its support of the minority Shi'ite *Huthis* in Yemen; and the party's support of the Shi'ite populace in Bahrain against the Sunni ruling dynasty might reverse the direction of the Arab Spring by spilling out into a bitter Sunni-Shi'ite discord (*fitna*), a probability that Hizbullah is fighting with its hands and nails to prevent at all costs. Would Hizbullah's massive arsenal deter such a possibility? How does Hizbullah's strong advocacy of Islamic unity comport with its seeming support of the Shi'ites against the Sunnis?

Is the Arab Spring limited by the opportunities it had provided? I am only ringing the bell in order to avoid a bad omen. As Prophet Muhammad said, '*Fitna* is hibernating /lurking in the dark. God damn those who wake it up'. Thus, vigilance must be exercised to ward it off at all costs. This might explain Nasrallah's initial comparison of the Sunni Al Khalifa ruling family in Bahrain to Sunni despots such as Mubarak and the late Qadhdhafi, and later on backtracking and retracting his statement, clarifying that his intention was just to highlight the 'oppression' (*mazlumiyya*) of the Bahraini people and the double standards of the international community that forced regime change in Libya, but is turning a blind eye and a deaf ear to the suffering of the Bahraini people. Concerning Syria, Nasrallah has called for a political solution to the conflict, not a military one, urging the Syrians to sit together at the dialogue table and stop violence and the language of guns. He also exhorted Western powers to leave Syria to its own devices, praising the 'balancing' role Russia and China are exercising in order to challenge American hegemony and put it at bay.[94] After more than four million refugees fled to Syria's neighbouring countries of Turkey, Jordon, Lebanon[95], and Iraq, the international community has done little to help. If a political settlement is difficult to be reached, then the efforts of the international community ought to converge on solving the humanitarian crisis. Still not enough aid is being delivered, and many Syrian refugees, especially children, are dying in the cold and suffering from malnutrition and diseases.

Conclusion

Hizbullah seems to be consistent in its discourse of maintaining its ideological alliance with Iran and its strategic-political alliance with Syria, as its 2009 Manifesto states.[96] The party is a strong advocate and practitioner of *realpolitik*. As a thoroughgoing realist, Hizbullah changes as circumstances themselves change: the party neither hesitates to go against the concept of popular sovereignty nor to interfere, or encroach upon, the sovereignty of other states, regionally (Syria) and internationally (Hizbullah's alleged 'terrorist activities' and 'global reach'[97]). It seems Hizbullah is facing the dilemma of asserting *raison de la nation* (pan-Arabism/pan-Islamism) or *raison d'etat* (state sovereignty). Most likely, its 'strategic' intervention in Syria has compromised both, including its ideology of supporting the 'oppressed' over the 'oppressor'. Through fuelling Sunni-Shi'a discord (*fitna*), Hibullah has weakened its pan-Islamic credentials by buttressing the state sovereignty of the Syrian regime at the expense of people's sovereignty. This seems to be in accord with the international community, which prefers a weakened Syrian autocratic regime to stay in power fearing the Islamists might win the fight. Most likely this is consistent with the Arab Uprisings, which lack a clear ideological vision, unified leadership, and institutionalization and constitutionalism. Asef Bayat argues,

The point is not to disparage the idea of radical revolutions, for there are many positive aspects to such experiences—a novel sense of liberation, free expression and open-ended possibilities for a better future being among the most obvious. Rather, it is necessary to highlight the fact that the revolutionary overthrow of a repressive regime does not in itself guarantee a more just and inclusive order. Indeed, radical ideological revolutions may carry in themselves the seeds of authoritarian rule, for the overhaul of the state and the elimination of dissent may leave little space for pluralism and broad political competition. By contrast, 'refolution' may create a better environment for the consolidation of electoral democracy because, by definition, it is unable to monopolize state power. Instead, the emergence of multiple power centres—including those of the counter-revolution—can neutralize the excesses of new political elites.[98]

Bayat concludes, "we might view the Arab uprisings as 'refolutions' or 'long revolutions' that may bear fruit in ten or twenty years by establishing new ways of doing things, a new way of thinking about power."[99]

Notes

1. The May 1916 Sykes-Picot Agreement between the British and the French carved Lebanon and the current Arab Middle Eastern states after the collapse of the Ottoman Empire. Joseph Alagha, *The Shifts in Hizbullah's Ideology*, (Amsterdam: Amsterdam University Press 2006) p. 21ff, 131.
2. Paul Viotti and Mark Kauppi, *International Relations Theory: Realism, Pluralism, Globalism*. (Boston: Allyn and Bacon, 1993) p. 583.
3. Paul Viotti and Mark Kauppi, *International Relations and World Politics: Security, Economy, Identity*. (New Jersey: Prentice-Hall, 1997) p. 352.
4. Raymond Hinnebusch and Anoushiravan Ehteshami (eds.), *The Foreign Policy of Middle East States*, (Boulder, Co.: Lynne Rienner Publishers, 2002), p. 353. See also Hans Morgenthau, *Politics among Nations*. (New York: Knopf, 1978).
5. Hinnebusch and Ehtieshami, *The Foreign Policy, p*1.
6. Ibid.

7. Ibid.
8. Ibid. p. 7.
9. Ibid.
10. Ibid.
11. Ibid. p. 9.
12. Ibid. p. 9-10.
13. Shibley Telhami and Michael Barnett (eds.), *Identity and Foreign Policy in the Middle East.* (Ithaca: Cornell University Press, 2002) p. 4.
14. Joshua S. Goldstein, *International Relations*, [Fifth Edition]. (New York: Longman, 2003).
15. Telhami and Barnett (eds.), *Identity and Foreign Policy,* p.182.
16. Ibid., 7, 63.
17. Alexander Wendt, "Collective Identity Formation and the International State", American Political Science Review, vol. 88 (June 1994), 385.
18. Hinnebusch and Ehteshami, *The Foreign Policy*, p. 2.
19. Ibid., 2, 45.
20. Telhami and Barnett (eds.), *Identity and Foreign Policy*¼, 169.
21. Irredentism refers to the "dissatisfaction with the incongruity between territorial borders and [Benedict Anderson's] 'imagined communities'." See Hinnebusch and Ehteshami (eds.), *The Foreign Policy…*, 7.
22. Hinnebusch and Ehteshami (eds.), *The Foreign Policy…*, 22.
23. Ibid., 336.
24. Ibid., 7ff.
25. Ibid., 7.
26. Ibid.
27. Ibid., 8.
28. Faleh Abdul-Jabar, 'The Structure of the State and the Arab Spring: A Sociological-Historical Approach', in: 'The Repercussions of the Arab Spring', the main session of *Al-Qarin's Nineteenth Cultural Forum*, 13-15 January 2013, pp. 3-24.
29. Barrington Moore, *Social Origins of Dictatorship and Democracy: Lord and Peasant in the Making of the Modern World.* (New Foreword by Edward Friedman and James C. Scott). (Boston: Beacon Press, 1993).
30. Abdul-Jabar, op. cit. pp 3-24.
31. Theda Skocpol, *States and Social Revolutions: A Comparative Analysis of France, Russia, and China.* Third edition. Cambridge: Cambridge University Press, 2013; and *Social Revolutions in the Third World.* (Cambridge: Cambridge University Press, 1995).
32. Interestingly, Hizbullah's leader Sayyid Hasan Nasrallah has repeatedly stated that he is for a 'strong, capable, and just' Lebanese state that inculcates deeply rooted democratic practices, rather than a weak state that is in constant "search

for optimizing its capacities amidst threats of dominion from powerful countries". Nasrallah called for "the empowerment of State institutions, the protection of sovereignty, and the realization of a genuine independence. In this framework, the Lebanese, with all their political forces, social factions, cultural elites and economic agencies, have a vested interest in safeguarding this modus operandi [of strong state] and subscribing to it…" See, Joseph Alagha, *Hizbullah's Documents: From the 1985 Open Letter to the 2009 Manifesto*. (Amsterdam: Amsterdam University Press. 2011) pp. 124-25.

33. History progresses through class struggle and opposition, with an emphasis on economy as the most important materialistic determinant factor.
34. Rentier states: "States in the Arab world are highly dependent on a source of revenue called by economists 'rent.' Economists define rent as income acquired by states from sources other than taxation. Some economists call states that are dependent on rent for a certain portion of their income 'rentier states'; others call them 'allocation states' because the states distribute the rent they receive to favored clients and projects." See James L. Gelvin, *The Arab Uprisings: What Everyone Needs to Know*. (New York: Oxford University Press. 2012) p. 7.
35. Juan J. Linz, *Totalitarian and Authoritarian Regimes*. Boulder, CO: Lynne Rienner Publishers, 2000.
36. Max Weber, *Weber: Political Writings* (Cambridge Texts in the History of Political Thought). Peter Lassman (ed.) & Ronald Speirs (trans.). Cambridge: Cambridge University Press, 1994.
37. Asef Bayat, *Life as Politics: How Ordinary People Change the Middle East*. Second Edition. Stanford University Press. 2013) p. 2
38. See Manuel Castells, *Networks of Outrage and Hope: Social Movements in the Internet Age*. (Oxford: Polity Press. 2012); John G Scott and Peter J. Carrington (eds.) , *The SAGE Handbook of Social Network Analysis*. (New York: SAGE Publications Ltd, 2011).
39. Jean Bodin, *On Sovereignty*. Cambridge: Cambridge University Press, 1992. Jean Bodin (1530-1596) wrote his treatise in 1576 in French, which could be translated as *Six Books of the Republic* or *Six Books on the State*.
40. Ghassan Salame, *Democracy without Democrats*. (London: I.B. Tauris, 1994.)
41. More than five secret face-to-face meetings where held between Iran and the US prior to the breakthrough deal. Deputy Secretary of State William Burns and Jake Sullivan, a key adviser of President Barak Obama, played a leading role in breaking the ice between Iran and the US. See Julie Pace, "Vanishing Adviser Reappears as Iran Policy Player", *Associated Press*, (23 December 2013): http://news.yahoo.com/vanishing-adviser-reappears-iran-policy-player-185811990--politics.html
42. Olivier Roy, *Globalized Islam: The search for a new ummah*. [Revised and updated edition] (London: Hurst and Company, 2004) pp. 58-99; see also, "Le Post-

Islamisme." *Revue du Monde Musulmans et de la* Méditerannée. (1999) pp. 85-86.

43. Farhad Khosrokhavar, "Le Hezbollah, de la Société Révolutionnaire a la Société Post Islamiste" (The Hizbullah: From a Revolutionary Society to a Post-Islamist Society), in Claude Gautier and Olivier Le Cour Grandmaison, (ed.),*Passions et Sciences humaines*, Paris: CURAPP, 2000), pp. 129-144.
44. Gille Kepel, *Jihad: The Trial of Political Islam*, Translated by Anthony F.Roberts. (London: I.B. Tauris Publishers, 2002), p. 368; see also Kepel, *Beyond terror and martyrdom: the future of the Middle East*, translated by Pascale Ghazaleh. Cambridge, MA: The Belknap Press of Harvard University Press, 2008).
45. Peter Mandaville, *Global Political Islam,* (New York: Routledge, 2007) pp. 343-348
46. Boubekeur, Amel. "Post-Islamist Culture: A new Form of mobilization?" *History of Religions*, 47, no. 1, (2007) pp 75-94.
47. Asef Bayat, *Making Islam Democratic: Social Movements and the Post-Islamist Turn*. (Stanford: Stanford University Press, 2007) pp. 10-13.
48. Mandaville, op. cit. p. 348)
49. Asef Bayat, 'The Coming of a Post-Islamist Society'. In *Critique: Critical Middle East Studies*, 9 (Fall 1996), 43-52.
50. Asef Bayat, *Islam and Democracy: What is the Real Question?* (Amsterdam: Amsterdam University press, 2007) pp. 17-20.
51. Ibid. pp. 20-21.
52. For instance, Hajj Muhammad Ra'd, member of Hizbullah's *Shura* (Consultative) Council and the head of the party's parliamentary bloc (personal interview, 27 December 2011).
53. Mandaville op. cit. pp. 343-8.
54. Neera Chandhoke, *State and Civil Society: Explorations in Political Theory*. (London: Sage Publications, 1995) p. 230.
55. Ibid., 233, 225.
56. Seteney Shami, *Publics, Politics and Participation: Locating the Public Sphere in the Middle East and North Africa*. (New York: Social Science Research Council of America, 2009) p. 37.
57. See Alexander Wendt, "Collective Identity Formation and the International State", *American Political Science Review*, 88 (June 1994), p. 385. See also Wendt's, *Social Theory of International Politics*, (New York: Cambridge University Press, 1999).
58. A reference to the *Shib'a* Farms and the occupied part of the *Ghajar* village. Alagha, *Hizbullah's Documents*, pp. 153-154.
59. Olivier Roy, "Islam: The Democracy Dilemma", in Robin Wright (ed.) *The Islamists Are Coming: Who They Really Are*. (Washington D.C.: U.S. Institute of Peace and the Woodrow Wilson International Center for Scholars, 2012), pp. 13-19.
60. Fayyad is one of Hizbullah's leading intellectuals. He is a professor of sociology

at the Lebanese University, the ex-director of the Party's think tank CCSD, and the drafter of the first part of the Hizbullah's 2009 Manifesto.

61. Muhammad Buazizi, a Tunisian street vendor, ignited the Arab Spring, when on 17 December 2010 he committed self-immolation in protest for the confiscation of his wagon. He succumbed to his wounds on 4 January 2011. This was the straw that broke the camel's back; the catalyst that triggered massive protests against the Arab autocratic, corrupt regimes, which were in power for decades.
62. Personal interview, Beirut, 15th May 2013.
63. Personal interview, Beirut, 30 May 2013
64. Personal interview, 14 May 2013. See also his articles in *al-Safir* (4 & 14 February 2012), and "*Nahwa Nazariyya Siyasiyya lil Tahawulat Al-'Arabiyya* [Towards A Political Theory for the Arab Uprisings]", in: Talal Salman et al., *Qira'at fi Al-Intifadat Al-'Arabiyya [A Reading in Arab Revolutions]*. Ma'lumat Vol. 90. (Beirut: Al-Markaz Al-'Arabi lil Ma'lumat, May 2011), pp. 109-114.
65. For instance, see Dale Eickelman, "New Media in the Arab Middle East and the Emergence of Open Societies", in Robert W. Hefner, (ed.) *Remaking Muslim Politics: Pluralism, Contestation, Democratization*. (Princeton: Princeton University Press, 2012) pp. 37-59; Jon W. Anderson, "Electronic Media and New Muslim Publics", in *The New Cambridge History of Islam*, Vol. 6 *Muslims & Modernity*, 2009; Gary R. Bunt, *Muslims: Rewiring the House of Islam*. (Chapel Hill, NC: University of North Carolina Press, 2009); John G. Scott and Peter J. Carrington (eds.), *The SAGE Handbook of Social Network Analysis*. New York: SAGE Publications Ltd., 2011; Manuel Castells, *Networks of Outrage and Hope: Social Movements in the Internet Age*. Oxford: Polity Press, 2012.
66. Lynch seems to concur with Olivier Roy's notion, namely that the Islamists did not change; rather, they altered their strategies and policies, and maybe modified their vision, in order to adapt to the wind of change resulting from the popular uprisings.
67. Marc Lynch, "The Big Think Behind the Arab Spring". *Foreign Policy* 190 (Dec 2011), pp. 46-7.
68. See Asef Bayat, *Making Islam Democratic,* p. 197; and his article: 'Paradoxes of Arab Refo-lutions', *Jadaliyya* (3 Mar 2011): http://www.jadaliyya.com/pages/index/786/paradoxes-of-arab-refo-lutions; also 'Revolutions in Bad Times', *New Left Review* 80 (March-April 2013): 47-60.
69. Asef Bayat, *Life as Politics: How Ordinary People Change the Middle East*. Second Edition. (Stanford, Stanford University Press, 2013).
70. Asef Bayat, 'Revolutions in Bad Times', *New Left Review* 80 (March-April), pp. 47-60.
71. Joseph Alagha, *Hizbullah's Identity Construction*. (Amsterdam: Amsterdam University Press, 2011).
72. The trigger was the 17 December 2010 self-immolation of Muhammad Buazizi, a

Tunisian street vendor, in protest for the confiscation of his wagon. He succumbed to his wounds on 4 January 2011.

73. This day is also significant in the modern history of Iran and South Africa. In Iran, on that day in 1979 the 'Islamic Revolution' led by Imam Khumayni was victorious. In South Africa, the late Nelson Mandela was released on that date in 1990 after serving 27 years in jail.
74. Personal interview, Beirut, 30 May 2013.
75. Noteworthy, in 2005 al-Saadawi ran against Mubarak just to prove that there is no democracy in Egypt, rather only state repression and intimidation. Mubarak's thugs forced her to cancel her press conference in which she was supposed to outline her election program. See Nawal Saadawi, *Inahu Al-Damm [It is the Blood (of the Egyptian Revolution)]*. (Beirut: All Prints, 2014). See also, *Al-Thawwrat al-'Arabiyya [The Arab Uprisings]*, (Beirut: All Prints 2013).
76. It seems history repeats itself. Qadhdhafi's violent crackdown and execution are reminiscent of Romania's president Ceauşescu and his wife's execution in 1989 after a short trial by the revolutionaries.
77. On 25 February, when al-Hadi was delivering his inaugural address, a suicide bomber from *al-Qa'ida* targeted his presidential palace killing 26 of his guards. The adamant al-Hadi delivered a strong message promising a 'war of attrition' against *al-Qa'ida* in Yemen, one of the poorest countries in the Middle East, where half the population lives under $2 a day. On 27 February 2012, president Salah abdicated to al-Hadi (See CNN and BBC World News of 21 to 26 February 2012).
78. For instance, see Nasrallah's speeches of 19 March and 7 April 2011. In his speeches of 24 February and 15 March 2012, Nasrallah backtracked and qualified his discourse, 'let the Bahrainis solve their own problems by themselves; we will not interfere'.
79. According to official statistics, the turn out was 57.4% of the registered voters. 89.4% gave a vote of confidence, while 9.9% voted against. (*SANA*, Syrian News Agency 27 February 2012). Many Christians disapprove of the new constitution because it stipulates that the president should be a Muslim.
80. The number of the observers would be gradually increased to reach 300. See http://www.un.org/News/Press/docs/2012/sc10609.doc.htm (accessed 14 April 2012).
81. Nasrallah gave his first interview to a Western network since the July 2006 war. The thirty-minute interview with the program entitled, 'The World Tomorrow' on *Russia Today*, was hosted by the notorious WikiLeaks' founder Julian Assange. Nasrallah revealed that his party had conducted talks with the Syrian opposition in an attempt to convince them to open the dialogue channels with the regime, but they were adamant. According to Nasrallah, the situation in Syria would unfold into one of two scenarios: either (1) dialogue and reform or (2) civil war, which is precisely what the US and Israel and some Arabs are working for, as he claimed. Concerning Lebanese

politics, Nasrallah clarified that his party is constantly shunning participation in any domestic infighting. Nasrallah added, 'Our priority remains the liberation of our occupied land and the protection of Lebanon from the Israeli menace'. http://www.moqawama.org/essaydetails.php?eid=23914&cid=199 (accessed 17 April 2013).

82. Well, I hope I am wrong. I argued that many Lebanese thought that the civil war ended after the 'two-year war of 1975-1977', even the Lebanese government removed the barricades separating the Eastern and Western parts of the war-torn Lebanese capital Beirut. This was only a lull, and bitter fighting resumed: starting with the 'battle of the hotels'; passing through the 1978 and 1982 Israeli invasions; the ousting of the PLO from Beirut in 1982; the 1985-88 'War of the Camps' between the 'Sunni' Palestinian refugees in Lebanon, on the one hand, and the secular 'Shi'ite' Amal and the Shi'a defecting brigades of the Lebanese Army, on the other; the Amal-Hizbullah control war from April 1988 to November 1990; and ending with the control war between the Christian militia of the Lebanese Forces and the Christian brigades of the Lebanese Army on 13 October 1990.

83. http://www.moqawama.org/essaydetails.php?eid=27814&cid=141#.UaXNXaFKSSo

84. See the review of my *Hizbullah's DNA and the Arab Spring*. (New Delhi: IFPS, University of Calcutta and KW Publishers (KW), 2013. (Hardcover: 370 pp). (ISBN-10: 9381904391; ISBN-13: 9789381904398) by Victoria Fontan, Head of the Department of Peace and Conflict Studies and Associate Professor at the United Nations-mandated University for Peace. *Peace and Conflict Review* 7.2 (Summer 2013): 96-97. ISSN: 1659-3995; http://www.review.upeace.org/ http://www.review.upeace.org/images/pcr7.2.pdf

85. See his interview with *OTV* on 3 December 2013, and his speech of 20 December 2013, commemorating the assassination of Hassan al-Laqis, a leading cadre of the Islamic Resistance, Hizbullah's military wing.

86. "Should the Party remain focused on Lebanon, should it risk its pan-Islamic aura, or should it engage in a proxy-war against the regional interests of Qatar and Saudi-Arabia, to the risk of giving into the *fitna* or division that it has always managed to avoid within a Lebanese context? … the *fitna* mentioned in US-embassy cables at the time of the US-led invasion of Iraq in 2003 is no longer a Washington-hoped divide and rule scenario, but a painful reality in Syria". Fontan, *Peace and Conflict Review*.

87. While in Belgium, 310 days with no government did not result in the paralysis of institutions and power vacuum. On the contrary, the workings/functioning of the political order remained intact and the livelihood of the people improved with a boost in the economy coupled with low taxation. Thus, people's living conditions improved.

88. Organization for the Prohibition of Chemical Weapons-United Nations Joint

Mission for the Elimination of the Chemical Weapons Programme of the Syrian Arab Republic. http://opcw.unmissions.org/Default.aspx?tabid=6576&language=en-US (Accessed 18 December 2013).

89. The five permanent members of the UNSC and Germany.
90. http://i2.cdn.turner.com/cnn/2013/images/11/24/iran.text.pdf (Accessed 18 December 2013).
91. See Nasrallah's interview with *OTV*: http://www.alahednews.com.lb/essaydetails.php?eid=88728&cid=149 (Accessed 3 December 2013).
92. On 2 October 2012, Politburo head of Hamas Khaled Mash'al said that Hizbullah supports the Syrian regime, the 'oppressor'; while Hamas supports the Syrian people (Free Syrian Army), the 'oppressed'.
93. See, http://www.ansaruallah.com/; https://www.facebook.com/ansaruallah.net; http://www.aa.com.tr/ar/news/107899; http://www.youkal.net/2012-12-02-14-05-23/24-25/200-2012-12-04-13-48-42 (Accessed 16 March 2013).
94. See his speech of 15 March 2012.
95. By the acknowledgement of the international community, there are one million and 50 thousand officially registered Syrian refugees in Lebanon (*LBCI*, 15 December 2013). On 15 January 2014, the Lebanese Caretaker PM Najib Miqati announced in Kuwait – at Second International Humanitarian Pledging Conference for Syria – that the Syrian refugees are estimated to number one-fourth of the Lebanese people (See Lebanese daily newspapers the next day).
96. Alagha, *Hizbullah's Documents,* pp. 129-131.
97. The US, Israel, Canada, and the Netherlands consider Hizbullah as a terrorist organization. The UK differentiates between Hizbullah's 'political wing' and its 'military wing', dubbing the latter as a terrorist organization. On 26 July 2013, the EU followed the UK's classification.
98. Bayat, "Revolutions in Bad Times," pp. 59-60
99. Ibid. p. 60.

6. Islamic Politics, Arab Spring and Turkish Model

Mehmet Ozkan

Introduction

Islamic politics is an endeavor to shape the destiny of its own while the persisting theories and geopolitical power configurations continue to argue otherwise. The Middle East has always been the centre of this very Islamic politics especially from the 19th century when modernization and colonization started to take place in the region. Each structural change in global politics has added a new dimension to this phenomenon. The latest of this has been the Arab Spring since December 2010, but most effectively since the 25 January process in Egypt.[1]

The Arab Spring and managing its direction is the most critical challenge for the Islamic politics – perhaps it will continue to be so in coming decades. As the developments unfold, both regional and international players have taken different approaches to the region and even some of them have fluctuated in their position with regard to developments on the ground.[2] Despite the failing account of the West in terms of defending values in the region – as in the case of 3 July 2013 coup d'état in Egypt – there are emerging examples in terms of doing politics without being anti-western and modern. One such example, the Turkish experience has been pointed as a possible direction by many in the region and beyond. This has enriched the debate; however, without contextualizing the current developments within the broader Islamic politics, there will be always some missing pieces in the puzzle. Taking up this challenge, this article intends to debate and periodize the modern Islamic politics, then to discuss the Turkish experience for the Middle East and the Third World.

Islamic Politics in the 21st Century

Following the July 3 military coup d'état in Egypt, the Syrian dictator Bashar al Assad, leaping at the opportunity, made a statement claiming that the developments in Egypt were a reflection of the exploitation of religion in politics.[3] Although this is not a meaningful statement by itself, it was a sign of re-appropriation of the classical Western approach in the region. After the coup in Egypt, the West has avoided describing the conflict in the axis of Islamism; however, recent developments in the region have brought along serious debates in the West and among the Islamists over the way of conducting politics in the Middle East. How should Islamic politics be read in the context of the latest developments? My argument is that Islamic politics arrives at a critical turning point due to the crucial event in the three key countries of the region: Turkey, Iran and Egypt.

Legacy of the Past

The modernization and secularization movements in the early 20th century commenced almost simultaneously in these three key countries of the Middle East. Their radical and top-to-bottom experiences generated alternative approaches and oppositions in each of these respective countries. While Islamic opposition groups shared common ground, they attempted to affect power or to be in power by adopting different strategies.[4] Following the 1979 Revolution, the Islamic movement came to power in Iran. Egypt experienced this only after the 2011 Popular Revolution. However, Morsi's term as President was interrupted by the military coup at the end of the first year of the Muslim Brotherhood in power. Turkey, on the other hand, followed a different path. The democratization process transpiring in the republic since 1950 transformed the Islamic movement in Turkey. In this case, the movement did not radicalize because it successfully carved a space for itself within the political system even though it was arguably limited.

Despite all these different practices, when it comes to doing politics, the Islamist actors in these three countries have begun to share the same fate as of June 2013. Hassan Rouhani was elected president in Iran; the

Gezi Park protests took place in Istanbul, Turkey; and the military coup followed in Egypt on July 3. These developments should be read as the beginning of a new turn in Islamic politics. This new period is forcing a generation of more comprehensive, sophisticated and holistic politics for Islamists. Before examining the main elements of this new period, it is useful to contextualize the transformation of Islamic politics since the 20th century.

The 20th century can be evaluated roughly in four categories in terms of Islamic politics.[5] The chief one of these is the first quarter of the 20th century in which politics was done reflexively to defend material-spiritual values against the Western colonial power. Due to the dismantling of the Ottoman Empire and deepening influence of colonialism in the Muslim world, Islamic politics embodied a reactionary tone.

Following the losses along the process, the second quarter of the 20th century, which may be regarded as the second period of the century, was a black period for Islamic politics. Muslims were not represented at the state level and pushed outside politics. Due to this alienation the movements prioritizing the protection of Islamic lifestyle and education were born. This was the main reason for the establishment of the Muslim Brotherhood in 1928 in Egypt. Similarly Turkish Islamic movements had no choice but to withdraw to the underground in the 1930s and the 1940s and adopt rather introverted policies because of the harsh conditions of the time to preserve the Islamic lifestyle.[6]

After the World War II, Islamic politics entered its third period where Islamic actors, slowly but surely, regained a momentum and began to resurface in the political arena. The establishment of Pakistan as an Islamic state, as well as Turkey's transition into democratic with the Democrat Party period, and most importantly the formation of the Organization of the Islamic Conference in 1969 were the first signs of Islam's appearance in the political sphere.[7] The fourth period was rather a testing phase for the awakenings of the previous periods. In this last period, which is the fourth quarter of the 20th century, the National Outlook tradition came to power in Turkey, as Algeria and Sudan more or less experienced their first Islamic political administrations. However, the Establishment both in these countries and in the West could not tolerate the situation; thus, their political presence were halted either by dragging into a bloody civil war, as in Algeria, or political instability. These experiences galvanized the role of the Islamic movements and gave birth to the fifth period.

In this phase, the Islamic actors came to the fore with an emphasis on democracy rather than religion, and adopted a rather liberal tongue in their discourse. It was a successful period in terms of political leadership experience. Especially, the success of the Justice and Development Party (AK Party) in Turkey blazed a trail in the debates over the Islam-democracy harmony and became a source of inspiration for the Islamic movements in the region.[8] Just as it was considered to be a successful period, a positive viewpoint regarding the future of the region formed in concert with the positive impact of the Arab Spring.

However, first the Gezi Park protests in Istanbul, Turkey, and then the military takeover in Egypt, created the need to re-evaluate the Islamic movements' way of doing politics. Again in the same period, Iran, which is pressurized by the international community, elected a religiously conservative but moderate leader as its new President; and this signaled that Iran too will try to change the way of doing politics, at least rhetorically.

In terms of the developments transpiring in these three countries, the period of May-July 2013 was one where the fates of all Islamic political groups coincided, just as was the case in the beginning of the 20th century.[9] Turkey, Egypt and Iran will of course follow different experiences in relation to their own historical processes. However, they currently share a common challenge as of now and that is the emerging reality of the insufficiency of coming to power through elections alone. The challenge is no longer winning the elections, rather to be able to produce and implement the policies effectively. What I mean by this is that governance at political level does not automatically translate into socio-economic domination or influence. This, of course, does not mean to overlook domestic processes and troubles unique to each country, but it is crucial to find the main vein of Islamic politics.

Characteristics of the New Period

One should clearly see in this new period that the West still does not trust the political actors holding Islamic traditions in the Middle East, and it does not know how to interact with them effectively either. It is unlikely to foresee a change in Western attitude towards these groups in the short term. As such, it is perhaps the responsibility of these Islamic groups to find a new political language, style and strategy in order to participate in national political leadership and sharpen their presence for political sustainability. A key factor in this reform should be applying a much needed inclusive approach to their style of governance.

This inclusiveness has two dimensions. First is the visibility and implementation of a comprehensive political attitude because the majority of the time, inclusiveness is quickly noticed by people in very personal and real matters. As such, by merely applying a more inclusive approach, it will be felt by people and generate a greater affinity. The second is related to the use of a formative/distinctive language on wide ranges of issue in efforts to control discourse that shapes the formation of politics. If the 21st century is an age where people mostly are informed or have shaped their viewpoints via the 140 character tweets on Twitter and via some sort of perceptions, then the management of these perceptions becomes one of the most important elements. This has been shown clearly in the aftermath of the Gezi Park protests in Turkey,[10] and it has become a must for Egypt since the 25 January.[11]

The second most important element of the new style of Islamic politics is prioritizing to develop the capability and means to implement a new type of politics that cannot only effectively use the political gains, but also shape the content, formation and the future of the politics within the country. From now on, if an Islamic movement is actually interested in governing rather than simply being "in power" politically, implementing what I call as *muqtader* politics is a must. What I mean by this is that not only focusing on getting to power by elections alone, but intensifying and prioritizing the policies that shape the social and economic dimensions of the politics. The recent developments in the region have clearly showed that nothing is guaranteed even if one comes to power by winning 50 percent of the votes; unless the top 50 richest men are conscientious and decent natives who do not take orders from anybody or any place. It is clearly seen that a political gain through ballots cannot shape and govern the social-economical dynamics unilaterally. Indeed, voting does not hold significance by itself.

Assertive and Comprehensive Politics

From this perspective, perhaps the real objective of the political actors having Islamic tendencies from now on should be influence over social-economic elements rather than coming to power through election processes alone. This is valid for the three key countries (Turkey, Egypt and Iran) of the region. Despite the fact that Islamic actors have been in power in Iran since 1979 Revolution, they have neither achieved inclusiveness nor shaped the social-economic order in the country. In a political sense, being in power is a serious gain since the Revolution, but it has somehow started to lose its value over society. In Turkey, the AK Party, after being in power for the last ten years, has seen through the Gezi Park protests that they are not really dominating the social-economic dynamics. This has been crystal-clear in the case of Egypt, where a democratically elected President has been ousted unreasonably by the military.[12] It is seen that there is no guarantee to maintain the rights claimed with the popular support.

In this framework, the developments that took place in 2013 have shown that the Islamic political actors from now on will assure political gains if and only if they achieve/demonstrate to have *muqtader* politics. Islamic politics has not come to an end, as Assad claims, but has faced the necessity of generating a new style. This new style should neither be defensive nor apologetic. On the contrary, it should be as assertive, as inclusive and as comprehensive as it can be. This is the fundamental point that the developments in the Middle East highlight.

Turkish Model and Islamic Politics

Although literally it might sound very true, in more than three decades, after the existence of Islamic-oriented National Order Party in 1969,

Turkish politics has been analyzed by many as if the Islamists are trying to get into power on the one hand, the secularists or state elite with the help of military is keeping the country's orientation toward the west in order to protect Turkey as a secular state on the other.[13] This image of Turkey, mostly established such contradictory analysis of Turkish domestic politics, has created more confusion to understand Turkey and its policies rather than contributing to understand as initially aimed.

An Islamist versus secularist understanding of Turkey has accelerated since the Refah Party entered the parliament as the biggest party after getting more than 21 percent of the votes in 1995 general election. After becoming coalition partner in 1996-97 with the True Path Party with the Refah leader Necmettin Erbakan as Prime Minister, Turkish political analysts have triggered the debate on Islamists versus Secularists. Although Erbakan was ousted from power with a "postmodern coup" in 1997, such debates never ended in academic and political circles.

However, with the coming of the AK Party, a split up from Islamist Refah Party, to power in 2002 with an absolute majority in the parliament, the discussions have focused on two issues. One is just to update the earlier debate regarding the secret intention of AK Party, if any, to move Turkey towards the Islamic world and the future of secular Turkey. The second debate has focused mainly on the modelhood of Turkey for the Middle Eastern countries, because of Turkey being a secular and democratic country with a Muslim population.[14] AK Party's coming to power has actually created a quiet, mild transition that is nevertheless radical in terms of its consequences.[15]

The analysis of Turkish politics as a clash between Islamists and Secularists is deeply flawed. Such an approach is neither helpful to understand Turkey fully nor advance the debate when it comes to its modelhood, if there is one. In Turkey, the main clash has always been between centre and periphery, rather than Islamist and Secularist. Islamist and Secularist positions just happened to represent centre and periphery, respectively, hindering the real conflicting sides. Turkey needs to be analyzed from the centre-periphery perspective and the Turkish model should be looked at as Turkey's normalizing of its domestic politics between centre and periphery.

Defining the Centre and the Periphery in Turkey

It is understandable that certain degree of cultural difference and distance between the elite (centre) and masses (periphery) in all societies due to historical, economic and political reasons might exist. However, such a distance between the centre, the secularist elite, and periphery, pious masses in Turkey has been particularly wide in the Republican area.[16] From the outset, the founders of the Turkish Republic were unable and often unwilling to establish effective channels of communication with the Anatolian-based periphery. They were remembered only when the votes were needed, during which most of the time the center resorted to use 'traditional and religious symbols' to win the hearts and minds of periphery.[17] Such strategy was temporary and was never able to establish a solid line between the two or to create an ideology of 'the popular mind'.[18]

As correctly argued, it is important to keep in mind that the cultural distance between 'centre' and 'periphery' was an important polarity even during the Ottoman period in political and economic life.[19] In short, the centre consisted of the civil, military and religious bureaucracy representing the state apparatus with the Sultan at the top, while the periphery included the local notables, peasantry and ordinary people. However, in order to grasp fully the change with the Republican Turkey, one needs to remember the state-society relations during the Ottoman period. From time to time, despite the tension between official and folk Islam, the Islamic nature of the political regime was crucial in providing legitimacy of the centre in the eyes of periphery. At that time Islam provided a common understanding, approach and a cultural bridge between the Ottoman elite and the society at large.[20] When it comes to the Republican area, there existed a new configuration of social actors and the modernist-secular centre became increasingly resentful of religiosity and Islam, and excluded Islamic elements from social life gradually and later on completely, if possible.[21]

1990s: Islamists as the 'Centre' of the Periphery

Mainly with the help of economic liberalization process in Turkey after 1980s, there has been a huge transformation in the periphery *per se* in terms of acting, thinking and looking at the issue. As the periphery gained more economic independence and freedom, it has proved itself by consequently electing *rigid* and seemingly contradictory political parties to power especially after the death of Ozal in the 1990s.[22] From economic organizations such as Independent Industrial and Businessmen Association (MUSIAD)[23] to youth organizations and to non-governmental organizations, the periphery has started to organize itself more powerfully and asked to be listened to. Started slowly in 1980s, after the 1990s the process started to bear fruit from intellectual, political and economic sphere and by merging with the already continuing of the same process, the result has become doubled. With the help and experience of the 80s generation, the process seemed to be accelerated. Indeed, the process was still slow, but the number of people who went through this process was increasing. This created instinctive reactions and fears among the elite of a centre that found its way in the expression of anxiety of losing hegemonic position.[24]

Against this background, the centre initiated counter projects to stop the 'marching of periphery' to the centre. The so-called 28 February 1997 process, which ousted Welfare Party from power in a bloodless coup, and its aftermath have shown such move clearly. The barring of girls wearing headscarf to enter university, and naturally shutting down of Imam Hatip High Schools by limiting the fields at university entry exam through which its graduates can pursue their further studies, together with the closing the doors of Welfare and its successor Fazilet (Felicity) Party, all was intended to serve one purpose: to prevent or slow down the process of periphery walking to the centre rather than preventing Islamists taking over the country. During such a politically chaotic environment, the election of Nationalist Movement Party (MHP) to the Parliament in the 1999 election as the second biggest party was not a surprise at all. Turkish society was searching the ways to channel its voice, anger and exclusion from politics, and the lotto, so to speak, went to MHP. Until the major economic crisis in 2000 and 2001, people in Turkey were still optimistic about their future. However, after the economic crisis, which drained such hopes down, the situation led people to look at new ways and faces in politics in the 2002 general elections.

Turkey's AK Party in Domestic and Regional Context

The result of the November 2002 election in Turkey should be seen as a turning point in Turkish political order.[25] If the rise of Islamist Refah Party in 1990s is seen as one of the most interesting characteristics of Turkish political system, an equally important noteworthy development is the existence of the AK Party.[26] The election of AK Party as a representative of isolated and excluded periphery with an absolute majority to the Parliament in 2002 and subsequent elections and its fast-track acceleration of the Turkey's EU process, whether it be influenced by external or domestic imperatives or both, have created possibility of a mild but radical exit from long-existing centre-periphery conflict in Turkey. In other words, AK Party has undertaken unwittingly the mission to complete or maturate Turkey's modernization process with the extension of democracy. The realization of the ending of centre-periphery *cul-de-sac* by a conservative party, the AK Party, not by the traditional westernizers like Republican Party (CHP), might finally lead the normalization ofTurkey's long-wanted modernization/Westernization adventure possible.[27]

It is commonly argued that the success or failure of the AK Party experience in Turkey is likely to have repercussions beyond Turkey's border and in the entire Islamic world.[28] In the literature, while analysis like 'secular Turkey stands out as the bright and shining model for democratic development across the Islamic world'[29] widely exists, it is not clear what kind of modelhood Turkey can offer to the Middle East or to the Islamic world. Similarly, as democratization is becoming a reality in Turkey with its overwhelmingly Muslim population, the answer to the question of what does this development have to do with the Islamic world in practical application is not clear. Then, the development of 'Muslim democracy' and its applicability to other places is becoming not more than an 'empty box' discussion, if this notion is not evaluated and understood within the social dimensions/structure of the Middle Eastern states.

Today in all non-democratic countries in general and in the Middle East in particular, there exists an alienated and excluded periphery that has almost no voice or influence in the decision making process; although the revolutions in the Arab world since 2011 is likely to change this in the longer term. Such groups usually resort to violence as the only way to express themselves, and come to surface sometimes as Islamist, sometimes as Leftists (or socialist) or another ideological form depending on the "opposition" ideologies of the time. If Turkey today with the AK Party's coming to power has consolidated or partly settled down its centre-periphery relations without civil war or one side using violence, there lies Turkey's modelhood to the Middle East and even possibly to the third world. Most of the problems in the Middle East have emanated from domestic sources rather than external ones. Naturally, the starting point to bring democracy, peace and prosperity should be there. A domestically-consolidated Turkey has much to offer to the Middle East where the centre-periphery clash is high. With the AK Party, the existing newer Turkey can be a much better model for the region and beyond.[30]

One important lesson to be learned from Turkey's experience for the Middle East is that while Turkey is consolidating it center-periphery relations, there exist relatively independent state institutions that allowed periphery to persist in the system, be it elections or competition with other. In Turkey there was an absolute control of centre on the state institutions until 1950s that automatically excluded periphery. After 1950s, day-by-day the control of Turkey's state institutions has been moved from the hand of centre (albeit still under the supervision of centre) to the middle between centre and periphery. The institutional character of Turkey made it relatively easy to keep Islamists from resorting to violence, and it has kept a way of 'hope' that one day they can rule the country. In the current Middle East, neither such an institutional structure that allows the periphery to have a 'voice', is to be found, nor is there any other way that the periphery can make itself be heard except resorting to violence.

State institutions are under absolute control of autocratic regimes, which is similar to the pre-1950 condition of Turkey. As experience from Turkish case, first an 'opening up' of institutions strategy should be implemented, then gradually pushing toward a more accommodative centre-periphery relation. Therefore, as Brumberg[31] rightly argued, "for democracy to have any hope in the Arab world, it is not Islam to be fixed, but politics itself".

Conclusion

Political issues and developments in the Third World have usually been looked at through the prism of theories and perspectives that might be seemingly fit to explain the issues. This article does not offer a new perspective for understanding the politics in the Third World, however, departing from the Turkish case, it argued that the analysis of Turkey from a secularist-Islamist clash perspective hinders the Turkish reality that exists for a long time now.

Analyzing Turkey through the prism of a clash between Secularists and Islamists has actually prevented outsiders (and even insiders) to see the issues from a broader perspective. Therefore, the Turkish case should be approached from a centre-periphery perspective, which I believe will help us to understand it much better. Looking from this angle, the AK Party experience in Turkey after 2002 needs special attention from several perspectives. First, its existence was the natural result of the newly developing and rapidly globalizing periphery in Turkey.[32] The AK Party has been supported by the periphery with an overwhelming support and intended to be the voice of periphery. In Turkish domestic politics, it has been the first party that has increased its votes in the election after first period in the office.

The importance and success of the AK Party has implications beyond Turkey. In almost every third world country and the Islamic ones in particular, there exists a centre who dominates the power and a periphery that is actually deprived of power and decision-making. For example in the Middle East, there is a distinctive division between the ruling elite and the public. What is striking is that due to lack of democracy and mostly the power transfer being held between family members, the excluded majorities have no way to channel their voices to be heard. AK Party is the only experience in the Middle East that brought the periphery to the centre without alienating or/ and clashing directly with the centre. This itself represents a major breakthrough given the existing literature's emphasis that Islam and democracy are incompatible. The AK Party example shows that both can co-exist peacefully with an increasing legitimacy from the public. In that sense, AK Party can be seen as a model in a way that it has consolidated Turkey's historical domestic divide between the centre and periphery. Considering that each society has different historical, institutional and structural setting in its political arena, the AK Party experience in Turkey can be an inspiring model in the Third World in general and the Middle East in particular. As the leaders behind AK Party experience made it explicit as early as in 2003 and later years frequently, Turkey does not want to be a model to any country, but drawing lessons and being 'a source of inspiration' in 'find[ing] their own solutions to their own problems' are as normal as historical events.[33]

Similarly the AK Party and Turkish experiences in Islamic politics represent the transformation from the fifth period to the sixth period in the modern Muslim politics. The fifth period has been relatively calm and successful. In the sixth period, there is likely to be more turbulence in Muslim countries, especially those in the Middle East as the Arab Spring has scattered the whole structure of politics and social dynamics. However, the success and failure of the key countries such as Turkey, Iran and Egypt will continue to shape Islamic politics in the years to come.

Notes

1. See Nurullah Ardıc, "Understanding the 'Arab Spring': Justice, Dignity, Religion, and International Politics", *Afro-Eurasian Studies*, 1 (1), 2012: 8-52.
2. For example on Turkey's policy toward the Arab Spring, see Mehmet Ozkan and Hasan Korkut, "Turkish Foreign Policy towards the Arab Revolutions", *Epiphany: Journal of Transdisciplinary Studies* 6(1), 2013: 162-181.

3. This part is an expanded version of Mehmet Ozkan, "A New Period in Islamic Politics", *YourMiddleEast.com*, 27 August 2013, http://www.yourmiddleeast.com/opinion/mehmet-ozkan-a-new-period-in-islamic-politics_17418
4. See Hasan Kösebalaban, "The Impact of Globalization on Islamic Political Identity: The Case of Turkey," *World Affairs,* Vol 168, No 1, 2005, pp.27-37.
5. More on this see Ahmet Davutoğlu, "Rewriting Contemporary Muslim Politics: A Twentieth-Century Periodization", in Fred Dallmayr (ed*), Border Crossings: Toward A Comparative Political Theory*, (New York, Lexington, 1999): 89-119.
6. For the experiences of Muslim politics see Nurullah Ardıç, *Islam and the Politics of Secularism: The Caliphate and Middle Eastern Modernization in the Early 20th Century*, (London & New York: Routledge, 2012).
7. On the dimension of the OIC, see Naveed S. Sheikh, *The New Politics of Islam: Pan-Islamic Foreign Policy in a World of States*, (London: Routledge Curzon, 2003); Mehmet Ozkan, "Turkey in The Islamıc World: An Instıtutıonal Perspectıve", Turkish Review of Middle East Studies 18, 2007: 159-193.
8. Burhanettin Duran, "Understanding AK Party's Identity Politics: A Civilizational Discourse and its Limitations", *Insight Turkey* 15(1), 2013: 91-109.
9. For an excellent comparative perspectives on Turkey, Iran and Egypt in the 20th century, see Alev Erkilet Başer, *Ortadoğu'da Modernleşme ve İslami Hareketler [Modernization in the Middle East and the Islamic Movements]*, (Istanbul: Yoneliş, 1999).
10. Hatem Ete and Coskun Tastan, *Kurgu ile Gerçeklik Arasında Gezi Eylemleri [Gezi Protests Between Fiction and Reality]* , (Ankara: SETA, 2013).
11. Mehmet Ozkan, Foreign Policy after Tahrir Revolution: (Re)-Defining the Role of Egypt in the Middle East. (Lap Lambert, 2011).
12. For the legacy of Mohammed Morsi in foreign policy, see Mehmet Ozkan, "*Egypt's Foreign Policy under Mohamed Morsi",* Ortadogu Analiz 5(51), 2013: 10-18.
13. This part is the expanded version of Mehmet Ozkan, "*Turkey, Islamic Politics and the 'Turkish Model'",* Strategic Analysis 37(5), 2013: 534-538.
14. Salim Cevik, "Myths and Realities on Islam and Democracy in the Middle East", *Estudios Politicos*, 38, 2011: 121-144.
15. The AK Party's coming to power has been analyzed from different angles, for example Gamze Cavdar sees from a *new thinking* perspective, "Islamist New Thinking in Turkey: A Model for Political Learning?", *Political Science Quarterly* 121 (Autumn 2006): 477-497; for a Muslim-Democrat party perspective Vali Nasr, "The Rise of 'Muslim Democracy'", *Journal of Democracy* 16 (April 2005): 13-27.
16. Omer Taspinar, *Kurdish Nationalism and Political Islam in Turkey: Kemalist Identity in Transition*, (New York: Routledge, 2005): 116.
17. Binnaz Toprak, *Islam and Political Development*, (Leiden: E.J.Brill, 1981): 37.
18. For the 'the popular mind' concept see Jack Snyder, *Myths of Empire: Domestic*

Politics and International Ambition (Ithaca, NY: Cornell University Press, 1991).

19. Serif Mardin, "Center-Periphery Relations: A Key to Turkish Politics?", *Daedalus* (Winter 1973): 70.
20. Taspinar, *op.cit.*, 118.
21. See Yildiz Atasoy, *Turkey, Islamists and Democracy: Transition and Globalization in a Muslim State*, (London and New York: I.B. Tauris, 2005), especially chapter 2.
22. Consider that in 1990s almost all ideological parties in Turkey have won an election and became part of a coalition: Islamist Welfare Party in 1995, Nationalist Action Party in 1999, Democratic Left Party again in 1999, Motherland Party and True Path Party in early 1990s. The 2002 election brought a completely new party to power, Justice and Development Party (AK Party). For the legacy of Özal in Turkish politics, see Muhittin Ataman, "Leadership Change: Özal Leadership and Restructuring in Turkish Foreign Policy", *Alternatives: Turkish Journal of International Relations*, 1, (1), 2002: 120-153; and Muhittin Ataman, "Özal Leadership and Restructuring of Turkish Ethnic Policy in the 1980s," *Middle Eastern Studies*, 38 (4), 2002: 123-142.
23. For MUSIAD, see Sennur Ozdemir, *MUSIAD: Anadolu Sermayesinin Donusumu ve Turk Modernlesmesinin Derinlesmesi [MUSIAD: Transformation of Anatolian Capital and the Deepening of Turkish Modernization]*, (Ankara, Vadi Publications, 2006).
24. Ahmet Insel's similar argument after the AK Party victory can be extended after 1980 process in general, "The AKP and Normalizing Democracy in Turkey", *The South Atlantic Quarterly* 102 (Spring-Summer 2003): 299.
25. See Ziya Onis and E. Fuat Keyman, "A New Path Emerges", *Journal of Democracy* 14 (April 2003):95-107; and Soli Ozel, "After the Tsunami", *Journal of Democracy* 14 (April 2003):80-94.
26. Ergun Ozbudun, "From Political Islam to Conservative Democracy: The Case of the Justice and Development Party in Turkey", *South European Society & Politics* 11 (September-December 2006):543.
27. Ahmet Insel argues that AK Party has a possibility to take Turkey out of September 12 regime. However he makes similar point regarding the normalization of Turkey's westernization process. See his "The AKP and Normalizing Democracy in Turkey", *The South Atlantic Quarterly* 102 (Spring-Summer 2003): 306.
28. For an example, see Ozbudun, op.cit., 555; Galip Dalay and Dov Friedman, "The AK Party and the Evolution of Turkish Political Islam's Foreign Policy", *Insight Turkey* 15(2), 2013: 123-139.
29. Thomas W. Smith, "Between Allah and Ataturk: Liberal Islam in Turkey", *The International Journal of Human Rights* 27 (Summer 2005): 307.
30. Analyzing Turkey's modelhood from a foreign policy perspective, Graham Fuller argues that the new Turkey with its independent foreign policy inclinations and sympathy to the Muslim world can be seen as a real model, "Turkey's Strategic

Model: Myths and Realities", *The Washington Quarterly* 27 (Summer 2004): 51-64, and his book, *The New Turkish Republic: Turkey as a Pivotal State in the Muslim World*, (Washington: U.S. Institute of Peace, 2007).

31. Daniel Brumberg, "Islam is not *the* Solution (or *the* Problem)", *The Washington Quarterly* 29 (Winter 2005-2006): 99.
32. See Hasan Kosebalaban, "The Rise of Anatolian Cities and the Failure of the Modernization Paradigm", *Critique: Critical Middle Eastern Studies* 16, (September 2007):229-240.
33. For example see Foreign Minister Ahmet Davutoglu's interview, *Al-Ahram Weekly* (Cairo), http://weekly.ahram.org.eg/2004/716/focus.html (10 Feb 2005); and Prime Minister Recep Tayyip Erdogan's interview, *Newsweek*, (May 12, 2008):68, and President Abdullah Gul, "Turkey's Role in a Changing Middle East Environment", *Mediterranean Quarterly* 15 (Winter 2004):2-7.

7. Islam and Popular Sovereignty: *The Turkish Experience*

Anita Sengupta

> Turkey, as one of the first non-western modern Republics and a key player in the modernization of the developing world has proved to be one of the most radical, spectacular and influential cases in this direction. But a fundamentally crucial problem is that the modernization model promoted by the Kemalist project was still a top down imposition with some unsolvable contradictions and dilemmas inherent within the system: the quasi military imposition of reforms while necessary as a revolutionary tool betrayed the principle of democracy: the nationalist ideology ran counter to its embracing of the universality of humanism and the elite led economic development generated social division. Populist political and religious forces have managed to recuperate and manipulate the claims from the 'bottom' of the society and have used them to their advantage. [1]

This passage from a collection of commentaries written for *Today's Zaman* by Ihsan Dagi cites from the opening speech of Hou Hanru, curator of the Istanbul Biennial, where Kemalism is analyzed from a critical perspective. Dagi notes the condemnation that this passage evoked is representative of the views of neo-Kemalists and their efforts at a top down revolution. Dagi argues that Hanru's position was hardly condemnable as it is generally agreed that the republican project of building a 'nation state' and making a 'new nation' out of the remains of the Ottoman Empire was an example of top-down modernization. He goes on to argue that it is a historical fact that these were not carried out in a 'democratic' regime but by a single party government through 'revolutionary' means. Democracy with its elementary mechanisms and institutions began in 1950, which is described by many Kemalists as 'counter revolution'. Such post Kemalist criticisms of Turkey's modernization process are not uncommon. Menderes Cinar, for instance argues

> Modern Turkey has not emerged as a result of an autonomous modernization process. It rather rests on the modernization 'offensives' of Kemalism, the official ideology named after the founder of the Republic Mustafa Kemal Ataturk. The still lingering legacy of the top down nature of Kemalist modernization can be defined as a continuous attempt on the part of the state elite to control, limit and even instruct the political sphere while 'modernizing' and 'democratizing' the polity.[2]

Since the 1990's post modern critiques of Kemalist modernity have been particularly visible in Turkish politics. It has been argued that one way to explain the ideological problems confronted by the People's Republican Party (*Cumhuriyet Halk Partisi*, CHP) created by Kemal and by the centre-left as a whole can be explained in terms of a crisis of Turkish modernity or Turkey's modernization project.[3] The centre-left continuously re-emphasized classical Kemalist modernity and took a dismissive and hostile approach to alternative conceptions of modernity. This was highlighted in their reflections on Islamism and the Kurdish and Alevi question. Of course, part of the problem lay with the notion of modernity itself and the idea that there are certain goals and values that could be considered 'universal'. Societal complexities and varying definitions of 'goals and values' meant that there was emergence of a plethora of movements that came to question or provide alternatives to the Kemalist modernization project. The ideological change was evident in the Justice and Development Party (*Adalet ve Kalkinma Partisi*, AKP) programme resulting in victory for the party in the elections of November 2002. The AKP brought with it a double promise: to accommodate growing demands for inclusion (from both Turkey's majority Muslim population and the country's subordinated minorities) and to marry Turkey's mainstream Islamist tradition and conservative political right with the programme of modernization geared towards accession to the European Union. Reevaluation of the actors and dynamics that have shaped the last decade, however, suggests that sustainable solutions to many complex issues remain unclear and "Islamism with a human face" is yet to make an appearance. It has been argued that in part this failure emerges from the nature of power structures within the CHP and AKP both of which remain authoritarian. [4] A deeper understanding of this would therefore need to take note of Turkey's political culture and institutional framework.

The Turkish Experience with 'Modernity'

Kemalism aimed at creating a 'modern Turkey' where attachment to 'traditional' issues like religiosity and ethnicity were perceived as irrational. The aim of 'Turkish' modernity was to create a Turkey that conformed to the principles of 'advanced civilization'.[5] The notion of an Islamic state was anathema to Kemal and his supporters. They viewed such a state as the way to maintain the status quo and perpetuate the backwardness of Turkey. For their part the Kemalists wanted to see Turkey transformed into a modern nation-state which, in the words of Kemal would 'live as an advanced and civilized nation in the midst of contemporary civilization'.[6] Such a nation would have to be secular and rational emphasizing science and modern education in order to create a modern industrial economy. Kemalism ascribed to the classical tenets of modernity which is generally conceptualized as a process where reason was the driving force of progress or in the words of Habermas, a process which sought 'a rational reorganization of everyday social life'. [7] The rationality that the Kemalist leadership sought for was to transform Turkish society from its feudal past to a bourgeois society. The attempt was to transcend the monarchical and imperial structures of the Turkish society and replace them with rational bureaucratic institutions under the rule of law within a nation-state. However, it has been argued, the insistence on modernization proved to be an ideological handicap both from a conceptual as well as a pragmatic point of view.[8]

In Turkey the Tanzimat reforms were combined with the ideas of Ziya Gokalp in the perception of what the modern state would be like. As a member of the Committee of Union and Progress, Gokalp had a significant influence on the development of Kemalist mindset. It has been argued that this was particularly true of his conceptualization of how society should be organized. [9] Gokalp saw Tanzimat reformist ideas as the acceptance and domination of the Empire by Western norms, ignoring native culture, which he believed was the binding element of a healthy and ethical society. On the other hand, he argued that all ideals and aspirations, personal or societal, should be subservient to the well being and interest of the Turkish state, which was culturally defined in terms of commonalities of language, feelings, aspirations and education, steering clear of any notion of ethnic and geographical identities. Having perceived common culture as the essence of 'Turkishness' Gokalp believed that all interests in society should unite to achieve this. Religion was seen as an important element, as an aid to societal solidarity.

In fact, the question of the changing role of Islam in a world challenged by modernization and secularization had been on the agenda of Ottoman intellectuals ever since the middle of the nineteenth century. The Young Ottoman Society founded by intellectuals and professionals in Istanbul in 1865, was indicative of such activities. However, due to the authoritarian character of the Ottoman regime open debate remained limited. The period leading up to the First Constitutional Period (1876-1878) signified a short lived exception. The Second Constitutional Period, following the Young Turk Revolution in 1908, was more promising. To begin with the leaders of the Committee of Union and Progress had no objection to criticism as long as it was not directed against their own immediate actions and policies. This period therefore represented an unprecedented upsurge of open public debate. However, due to internal conflicts, the 1908 revolution could not live upto the heightened public expectation. Repeated attacks against the new regime forced the Committee of Union and Progress away from power for a short period in 1912. By staging a coup in 1913, they retrieved political control. Thereafter the Committee, under the leadership of Enver, Talat and Cemal held on to power till they escaped to Odessa after the Mudros armistice in 1918.[10]

Starting from the early 1920's when the Turkish state emerged as the Ottoman Empire's successor, the men who had led the military campaign against the Greeks were concerned with the creation of a state based on a different set of principles. Believing that they had 'to create a modern, therefore western state in Turkey', Kemal and his followers, mainly former military officers were eager to announce to the people and the world community that the old system of arbitrary relations between the ruling elite (*askeri)* and the *rea'ya*, the tax paying subjects of the empire who were excluded from politics would be abolished. In its place the western idea of citizenship would be firmly established as the new principle responsible for regulating the relationship between the elected, constitutionally limited rulers and 'the people'.[11] Kemal Karpat however argues that the evolution of events revealed that the transformation of the *rea'ya* into the people as sovereign was not the highest priority of the reformers.[12] Aware of Turkey's weak military and financial condition and the limited appeal of its pro-western ideas to the uneducated rural and religious oriented population, they concentrated their attention on the construction and function of the country's political institutions. A 'socialist democracy' was proposed which would be supportive of individual and associational pluralism, guaranteeing full expressional rights. The adoption of *halkcilik* or populism was a reflection of Gokalpian influence. With this in mind, six principles or guidelines were put in place; republicanism (*cumhuriyetcilik*) secularism (*laiklik)* nationalism (*milliyetcilik*) populism (*halkcilik*) statism (*devletcilik*) and revolutionary-reformism (*inkilapcilik*). These guidelines were incorporated into the programme of the ruling CHP in 1931 and its constitution in 1937.

The political leadership that emerged after the War of Independence was also radically secularist. Of all the different opinions regarding which civilization to identify with, it was the most radically western conception that became the prevailing one. Part of the reason was the war itself. The victory of the Turkish army was because of those sections of the army that had the best training according to modern standards had succeeded in taking control. The officers trained in military colleges based on the western model were naturally more inclined to modern and European values than were other groups. Ever since the Balkan Wars, the political power had been in the hands of the military leaders. Mustafa Kemal emerged out of the War of Independence as a very successful commander and as he belonged to the more radical Westernizers this partly explains the direction that politics assumed. A few years after the 'modern' Turkish Republic were established a reform programme based on secularism or laicism was implemented. Changes were carried out in the judicial system, in education, in the script and in headgear and clothing. While the 1924 constitution had stated that the 'religion of the Turkish state is Islam' this clause was deleted in an amendment made in 1928. To stress the secularist character of the state even more strongly, the principle of secularism was added to the constitution in 1937.

One field where secularism was particularly effective was the field of education. The old Islamic institutions, the *mektaps* and *medersas* were closed in 1924 and incorporated into a new and unified system of public schools under the Ministry of Education. The law that put this into effect was *Tevhid-i-Tedrisat Kanunu*. Religious education was put under the charge of the Ministry and a new Faculty of Theology was set up at the Darulfunun (the University of Istanbul) in 1924. In addition special schools were opened for the training of *imamas* and *hatips* in Istanbul. Interest in this new form of Islamic education never took root and in 1933 the Faculty of Theology was closed down and turned into an Institute for Islamic research. Typically in 1926, there were twenty schools for *imams* and *hatips,* in 1932 only two were left, one in Istanbul and one in Koyna. Likewise the number of students in Imam Hatip Schools was reduced to ten from 2258 in 1924. In public schools religion was taught in primary and secondary sections, but after the third Congress of the Republican Peoples' Party (CHP) in 1931 where the principle of secularism was included in the Party programme, it was declared that religious education was the responsibility of the family not the state. As a result religion was abolished from the primary and secondary school curriculum in 1935 and not reintroduced till 1948.

In the inter-war years official secularism was not based on atheism. Rather it represented a western ideal about modern religious piety which was individualistic and showed little external manifestation. The kind of religiosity that the Kemalists defended came close to this pattern. In recent times there have been certain changes in the system of education. With the AKP government coming to power there were efforts to end the inequalities in the education system where students from religious high schools had points deducted from the results of their university entrance exams effectively barring them entry to the country's most prestigious universities. Part of the military crackdown on political Islam introduced in 1999, it led to large numbers of students dropping out of religious schools. In July 2009 a decision was adopted by the Supreme Education Council to make it easier for students at religious schools to attend university. This is being identified as reflecting the changing balance of power in Ankara. [13]

Similarly, a programme was initiated by the Kemalists for the reformation of religious practices. A commission was set up with instructions to purify, simplify and intellectualize mosque services. A very significant part of this process was language. Turkish was to be the language of all ritual worship. In fact authorities succeeded in making Turkish the language for the call for prayers, thereby enforcing the unpopular inhibition against Arabic until the political liberalization in 1950. In November 1925, all male Turks were compelled to abandon the fez and wear in its place a hat with a brim, thereby ending social and religious distinctions which had been obvious from a person's headgear. This was followed by the introduction of a new calendar. Until 1917 the Turks had used three different methods of dating; the lunar Islamic system which began with year one in 622 AD when Prophet Muhammad migrated from Mecca to Medina; the modified Julian calendar with a 13 day difference with the Western Gregorian; and the Gregorian calendar which was used for official purposes. In March 1917, the Unionists introduced a modified Gregorian calendar with the traditional years retained. The Kemalists ended the confusion by adopting the Gregorian calendar which went into effect on 1 January 1926.[14] The Islamic way of keeping time with the new day beginning with the evening prayer made way for the international clock. These changes were made to facilitate communication with the outside world, especially regarding business matters. For the same reason, in 1935, Sunday was made the weekly holiday bringing the Turkish working week in line with the West.

The Arabic script was replaced by the Latin in the writing of Turkish. The Arabic-Persian letters had come to be seen as unsuitable for writing Turkish and blamed for the low level of literacy of the Turks. Reformers had considered simplifying the alphabet so as to make Turkish easier to read and write. Enver Pasha who had become Minister of War in 1914, produced an alphabet to increase literacy in the army. But few had considered abolishing the script and replacing it with a new one. By the early 1920's, however, there was a precedent when in 1924, the Soviet government decided to replace Arabic letters with Latin in the Turkic republics. The matter was debated in Turkey, throughout the 1920's. As a trial western numerals replaced Arabic numerals in May 1928. On November 1, 1928, Parliament passed a law introducing the new Turkish alphabet which was to be used in all publications from the beginning of the New Year.

Sufism has played a significant role in the history of Islam and in Turkey the Nakshbandis, the Mevlevis and the Alevi-Bektashi developed close relations with the state at various times. As discussions concerning the question of Turkish nationality intensified at the beginning of the twentieth century, the Young Turks turned to the Alevi-Bektashis for support. Their stress on Turkish identity appealed to the new ideological currents. Many of them saw the modern nationalism under Kemal as a chance for better relationships between themselves and the state authorities. The prohibition against all *tarikats*, including those of the Bektashis therefore marked a setback. By tradition, common people had been more closely attached to the Sufi *tarikats* than to the *ulema*. The secularizing reforms, in the fields of law and education, through which the power of the *ulema* was reduced therefore did not concern ordinary people too much. It was different with the reforms aiming to secularize daily life. Prohibition of the *tarikats* and closing of the *tekkes* (lodges) and *turbes* (shrines of saints) meant that places of popular worship were closed and this caused resentment. For most of the people loyalty to the nation did not prevent strong religious feeling. However, as modernization progressed the contradiction between republicanism and Islam posed questions which itself led to a new phase of development in the relationship between popular Islam and official secularism.

During the period following the Second World War, Turkey, like many other countries all over the world underwent a process of social and economic change. As a result of mechanization of agriculture, industrialization and the extension of infrastructure and of communication followed by a high rate of urbanization. As people became increasingly urbanized the character of popular Islam also changed. By the 1950's there was also a softening of official attitudes. In March 1950 a number of mosques that had been closed since 1925 were opened for prayers. This liberalization accelerated after the elections and in June 1950, a month after the democratic party had celebrated its election victory, the law requiring the *ezan* to be read in Turkish, rather than Arabic was changed. In 1969 a pro-Islamic political party was set up despite the fact that the law forbidding the 'use of Islam for political purposes' was still in force. Over the years the number of issues over which the secularists and the Islamists contended was also reduced. However, a number of issues continue to remain contended. One is the principle of secularism in the constitution, which according to Islamists contradicts the democratic spirit of the constitution. The second is the issue of Friday prayers. A third and the most controversial in recent times has been the issue of the headscarf.

The Kemalist model of modernization had a number of achievements to its credit. [15] It was able to accomplish significant industrialization and economic development. Within the broad parameters of this modernization project Turkey was also able to establish the key institutions of representative democracy. By the 1990's however, the Turkish model of modernization had reached an impasse. On the economic front the pace of development was not enough to produce a dramatic increase in living standards that would produce rapid convergence to west European norms over a short period of time. Turkey experienced a dualistic pattern of economic growth involving a co-existence of rich regions with substantial pockets of poverty in the presence of rapid population growth. On the political front, the existing democratic order failed to accommodate societal demands for greater recognition and participation. The interpretation of secularism and national identity followed by the Kemalist state restricted the capacity of the state to incorporate the demands of groups who wished for an extension of the boundaries of the political space on grounds of religious and ethnic identity. Hence, by the end of the 1990's Turkish modernization was confronted with two major challenges. First, there was the need to reform the "soft state" in the economic realm so that economic development could proceed more rapidly and equitably without costly crisis and interruptions. Secondly there was a demand to reform the "hard state" in the political realm, creating a space for political opening for those groups that favoured an extension of religious freedoms or the practice of their minority rights within the broad parameters of a secular and unitary nation state.[16]

A major problem that the model posed was the role of the military in Turkish politics. As Idris Bal notes the role of the Turkish army as an integral part of the Turkish Model is complicated.[17] The Republic was established by Generals (Ataturk and his colleagues) and it was ruled by another general, Inonu till 1950. Also most of the Turkish Presidents have been of military origin. Since 1950 the process of democratization in Turkey was interrupted four times during its short history in 1960, 1971, 1980 and February 1997. Yet in the 1990's Turkey enjoyed a multi-party democracy, a market economy and was in general proud of its armed forces. All the interventions were made with the intention of stopping the government from using religion as an instrument of party politics and 'adjust the balance of democracy'. The involvement of the Turkish Army in domestic politics has been encouraged by various factors. Turkish military Janissary tradition encourages the army to intervene in politics and this was strengthened by the fact that the national hero was a General. The Turkish army carries the image of being the initiator of reforms since reform in education started with the army. The Turkish army believes that its mission is to defend the state not only from external threats but also from what they consider to be internal threats and regards itself as the guardian of democracy. Also the Constitution and the administrative structure of the state have encouraged the military to intervene in politics. A lack of belief in the capacity of the civilian society to solve its own problems has also encouraged the military to intervene.

Another flaw of the Turkish model has been its understanding and application of democracy. This is reflected in its policies towards its minorities a fallout of which has been what is now identified as the state's policy towards the Kurds or the *Kurt Sorunu*. The Kemalist modernity project was oriented towards a particular vision of a 'modern' Turkish state which had attempted the transformation of a multicultural multilingual society into a nation 'happy to call itself Turkish'. The aim of 'Turkish' modernity was to create a Turkey that conformed to the principles of 'advanced civilization' where attachment to 'traditional' issues like religiosity and ethnicity were perceived as irrational. The attempt was to transcend the monarchical and imperial structures of the Ottoman society and replace them with rational bureaucratic institutions under the rule of law within a nation-state. However, it has been argued, the insistence on modernization proved to be an ideological handicap both from a conceptual as well as a pragmatic point of view. And one of the fallouts of this has been the Kurdish issue. Similarly the dissatisfaction of the Alawite religious minority appears as a potential cause for crisis. The inability of the state to recognize the Alawites as a separate group within the state has led to the comment that the model has not matured over the years.[18]

The Turkish Experience with Secularism

While perceptions and connotations have differed there is a broad consensus on the fact that the Turkish model is essentially based on its secular character. It has been argued that Turkish secularism was not about the separation of state and religion but about the submission of religion to the reason of the state, promotion of an acceptable 'state Islam' and the judgment of non-conforming Islams as potential threats to the 'secular' regime.[19] Hence secularism in Turkey involved not only the disestablishment of Islam, but also its different establishment in accordance with the new basis of legitimacy of separation of religion and state. Generally, the *sharia* is accepted as the main source of legislation in the Muslim world and there is stipulation that political parties should not conflict with the *sharia.* In Turkey on the other hand, Islam is legally irrelevant to political activity in the sense that considering it in law making is prohibited. The Turkish Constitution forbids the basing of fundamental, social, economic, political and legal order of the state on religious tenets. Another striking peculiarity of Turkish Islamism is the tradition of Sufism that has provided an outlet for Islamic religious expression and in doing so has blocked the radicalization of religion.[20] The Nakshbandi order does not visualize the state as an enemy and therefore does not produce a kind of antagonism that radical Islamists have adopted in other parts of the Islamic world. Largely influenced by this Sufi tradition, Turkish political Islam chose to participate in the electoral process hoping to affect change within the existing political structure. It also kept itself away from violence and terrorism with the minor exception of the Hezbollah, which according to Menders Cinar and Burhanettin Duran, should be analyzed in the context of Kurdish nationalism and the armed separatism of the Kurdish Workers Party (PKK) rather than Islamist movement.[21]

It is further argued that Turkish Islamism has been a local and nationalist phenomenon with little impact on and from Islamist movements elsewhere. More importantly, it has been argued, Turkish Islamism has been under the pervasive influence of Turkish nationalism with little organizational linkage to the Arab world. [22] The dissociation with Arab Islam dates back to the Ottoman bureaucratic center's condescension towards Arabs. This was continued in the Young Turk's suspicion of Arabs as secessionist and the perceived Arab betrayal during the First World War. Nationalism provided Turkish Islamists with a shield and vehicle for the expression of Islamist demands, because in the secularist Republican era openly Islamist movements that call for the application of the *sharia* were strictly forbidden. Therefore the call for the application of the *sharia* has not been a political slogan to be rejected or to be defended in the Turkish political system. Also although Turkey fought a War of Independence, Turkey has never been formally colonized. The War was fought by a coalition of Islamist, nationalist and leftist groups under the leadership of Mustafa Kemal Ataturk who later founded the secular-nationalist Turkish Republic. Although the war was waged on the basis of a predominantly Muslim identity, Islam was not the exclusive source of mobilization in the liberation of the country. Since Turkey had never been colonized it never joined the third bloc during the Cold War and had stronger orientation towards the West. The anchoring of Turkey into western structures has had an impact on its international trajectories. Although Turkish Islamism had some level of anti-western feeling due to the war of Independence and the Ottoman political experience with the West, the leading elements of Turkish Islamism abandoned their anti-European discourses in the 28 February Process and supported Turkey's integration into Europe.[23] It has been suggested that this change of mind can be related to the Islamist conviction that the process of transition into the EU is likely to force the Turkish political system to undertake significant democratic reforms that will make the Kemalist ideology less repressive and intrusive.[24]

Another feature that explains the specific evolution of Islamism in Turkey and its approach to the secular regime and democracy is closely bound up with the state dominant nature of Turkish political culture and tradition. [25] The Turkish Islamists' conception of the proper strategy necessary to soften the strict nature of Turkish secularism is a pragmatic and long term one. Here when the secular regime weakens its oppressive nature Islamists attempt to enlarge the sphere of their activity. When conditions worsen they show little resistance. This 'state dominant' character is also the reason why Islamists do not resort to violence when they are faced with repression. Turkey's Islamism can also be differentiated in terms of its diversity. As Turkish modernization unfolded, the Islamist movement diversified into a variety of political, economic, cultural and religious dimensions and manifest itself in various organizations from religious orders to human rights associations. [26]

In Republican Turkey, the Islamist movement passed through several stages. It was influenced by the unfolding of the modernization project, by the dominant ideological frameworks of the time and by the flexible nature of Kemalism. Kemalism has been defined as an anti-political state centred paradigm that claims that the Turkish society and public sphere is homogeneous and displays distaste for political representation of difference. In Turkey Kemalism was an institutionalized foundational ideology that was elevated to the status of moral consensus with the protection of the military. [27] The Turkish foundational ideology was one of controlled modernization. However, it failed to come to terms with the contradictions between Kemalism and Westernism, liberalism and national unity and democracy and secularism. Cizre-Sakallioglu argues that historically the Turkish state adopted a double discourse. On the one hand it established a rigid segregation between Islam and the political realm and on the other accommodated and incorporated Islamic polities into the system in various ways. [28] The leaders of the War of Independence that later established the secular Republican nation-state had employed an Islamic vocabulary in the struggle to liberate the nation. After the establishment of the Republic, a distinction was made between regressive and progressive Islam and the latter was promoted by the state as compatible with its modernization drive.

The dualism between Islam and secularism was also evident in the relations between the state and the minority in the 1920's in the course of defining Turkishness. Here, Kemalists were inspired by Zia Gokalp in the usage of the word culture or *hars*.[29] According to Gokalp the nation was a community of individuals united by a shared culture, based on common education, morality, socialization and aesthetics. Gokalp defined the nation through its collective values. Hence the word culture in the documents of the CHP, referred to the common past and mores (i.e Islam) of the Ottoman Turkish Muslims in Anatolia as well as their education and socialization in Turkish. For Gokalp, Islam was not only a faith, in its nominal form it was also a particular set of belief systems and mores that dictated the routines of daily life and socialization for the Muslims. Accordingly Islam could serve as a culture as well as an identity for the Muslims.

With the transition to competitive politics, a reciprocal relationship was established between Islamic groups and right wing political parties. The instrumentalization of Islam continued till the early 1990's and a pragmatic outlook dominated all religious formations at the level of the state and formal polities. While the practice of secularism had somewhat relaxed since the beginning of the multi-party regime its original state centred and control oriented definition was maintained by all Islamic groups, political actors and the state. Within the scope of secularism, the state's attitude towards Islam has varied considerably. As a result of the dual nature of Kemalism Islamist outlooks have been integrated into the political processes, but their presence has been problematized as reactionist internal enemies of the secular Turkish Republic. However, by the late 1990's the fact that the political elite needed to 'learn to live with Islam' was clear. Mustafa Erdogan, Professor at the Haceteppe University in Ankara argues that if Turkey wished to be democratic it could do so successfully only with Islam, not by attempting to cast it off. Indeed its history forces Turkey to be a 'Muslim Democracy'. [30]

The National Outlook Movement has been the most powerful representative of political Islam since 1970's.[31] The National Outlook Movement (NOM) and its first political party the National Order Party (*Milli Nizam Partisi)* were founded by Necmettin Erbakann with the support of some Sufi orders. After the closure of this party by the Constitutional Court during the 1971 military intervention the movement was reincarnated as the National Salvation Party (*Milli Selamet Partisi*) which was closed by the 1980 coup administration. The NOM mainly addressed socio-economic problems by employing an Islamic language and offering an Islamic morality as a panacea to them.[32] The third party of the NOM the Welfare Party (WP) maintained a secular emphasis on the problems of daily life and decided to broaden its support base and focus on more pragmatic requirements like equal distribution of consumer opportunities. It was however, during the period of the WP (1983-96) that Islam became a major player in Turkish politics. In 1994, the Party won the municipal elections in Istanbul and Ankara. In 1995, the Party received the highest share of votes (21.3%) and eventually managed to form a coalition with the centre-right True Path Party (*Dogru Yol Partisi*) TPP and make its leader Necemmetin Erbakan the Prime Minister of Turkey. It has been suggested that the WP-TPP coalition government represented a head on clash of Islamism and secularism and became a watershed in Turkish politics.[33] Since then in an ongoing military led secularist campaign, the military assumed a more active role in the making and ousting of governments. The WP and its successor the Virtue Party (*Fazilet Partisi* VP) were closed by the Constitutional Court on the grounds that they violated the principle of secularism. The WP's failure has been attributed to the fact that it disregarded the plural patterns of ideas, beliefs and lifestyles in society by attributing an Islamic essence to them and insisting that every Muslim should practice Islam in the way that the WP defined. It failed to come to terms with the fact that a majority of the Turks do not practice Islam in the way the party hoped. This led to polarization and an inability to counter the challenge of the military led secular establishment by broadening its constituency and or demystifying its alleged reactionist threat.

The failure of the WP to survive in power led to a change in strategy and tactics as well as discourses and visions of the WP. This change was partly due to the strict measures of the February 28 Process. But it also had to do with the recognition that democratization allowed the practice of Islam in daily life. A new party, the AKP was founded in 2001. The leaders of the party have stressed that they are trying to forge a new understanding of politics free from the politicization of religion. The roots of this second phase of Islamism, where a new generation of Islamists changed their rigid ideological corpus can be traced to a series of changes within Turkish Islamism in the 1990's. In the early 1990's Turkish Islamists started to redefine and reframe their religious demands and ideals in terms of a universal vocabulary on human rights and liberties. A significant factor here was the expectations and needs of the newly rising bourgeoisie and their economic interests which were directly related to the European markets. Apart from these the AKP's new discourse was also a culmination of transformation in the various Islamic sectors in Turkey from religious orders to intellectuals. Signs of this transformation can be found in the Fethullah Gulen Movement and the *Hak-Is* Labour Union. The Gulen Movement declared that Turkish integration within the EU would not result in cultural assimilation for Turkish society. Similarly the *Hak-Is* Labour Confederation successfully used the discourse of civil society to improve the interests of the workers. The transformation is probably best exemplified by Tayyip Erdogan's statement that "my reference is Islam".[34] However, it has been argued that Islam as a reference might take different interpretations. A reference to Islam can be at a personal level but also at the social or state level.

In the general elections of 3 November 2002, the Felicity Party (*Saadet Partisi*) which represented the National Outlook Movement (NOM) and was regarded as having strong Islamist views made a very poor showing (2.5% of the total votes). On the other hand the AKP, a breakaway group which was considered to be moderately Islamist received 34.3% of the votes and got 363 of the possible 550 seats in the Parliament. Ahmet Yildiz argues that this can be explained by the fact that the Turkish voters tend to adopt religious identity as a social common denominator and tend to distance themselves from political Islam and that they prefer that Islam does not assert itself at the political level. Therefore, he argues, the success of the AKP was based on its emphasis of adherence to the ideological creed of the Republic and claims to be a conservative democratic party not an Islamic one.[35] This was claimed as the mark of distinction that assured the 'legitimacy' of its political governance. The AKP has had a history of reaching out to the broader centre-right, of making room in its parliamentary group and in government for more secular conservatives and for Turkish nationalists. The strategy of coalition building is what principally distinguishes the AKP from its Islamist predecessors, and which has sustained its claims to being a centrist force. However, it is argued, that in reality preference is given to electing people for posts in the bureaucracy from those with a background in the National Outlook Movement. [36] It has been argued that the May 1, 2009 reshuffle of the cabinet, the first since the AKP came to power in 2002 signals that the party is intent on reasserting the party's conservative core.[37] This in itself is interesting since the leader of the NOM, Necmettin Erbakan, has claimed that it is the Felicity Party that represents the NOM and not the AKP. Based on this Ahmet Yildiz argues that the AKP is not the heir of the Welfare-Felicity Party but rose in reaction to it and as a breakaway party it drew a different line for itself in the political arena.

Moreover, it has been argued that since the AKP is the product of its members' past experience its Islamic connection is beyond question. This is a connection that some analysts label as 'new Islamism'. This 'new Islamism' is not power centred in the way that the NOM was. For the NOM acquisition of political power was the key to all social transformations and Islamic aspirations, which is not the case for the AKP. For the AKP, Islamization is not to be achieved through the state. The state is important only for opening new spaces for individuals and society as a whole by assuring basic rights and liberties. The state should not impose its ideology on society. 'New Islamism' aims to engage in politics on the basis of social legitimacy and socio-economic compromise. Change is achieved by liberating societal dynamics` and allowing them to be reflected in politics. With respect to world politics, 'new Islamism' reflects a reevaluation that sees civilizational dialogue between the Islamic and the western worlds as essential. Globalization has become a constant point of reference for the AKP leadership and the European Union is seen as its embodiment. Domestically, 'new Islamism' has developed a culture of compromise. As a result the leadership has refrained from political polarization and has distanced itself from insisting on solving issues that that could generate strong polarization. As such the AKP represents a compromise between democracy and Islamic identity and the management of tensions by peaceful means.

A new term 'conservative democracy' is being used to define the 'new Islamism' of the AKP.[38] Since its foundation the AKP leadership has argued that that politicization of religion is dangerous for democracy and religion. This is based on the awareness that the majority of the Turkish population is as strongly attached to democracy and secularism as they are attached to religious values. The 'new politics' is the search for a new social contract between different sectors of the Turkish society. It is based on a synthesis between liberal desires for reform and conservative cultural sensitivities. This was based on a three layered strategy: first, the adoption of a 'language of human rights and democracy as a discursive shield'; second, mobilization of 'public support as a form of democratic legitimacy'; and third the construction of a 'liberal democratic coalition with modern/secular sectors that recognize the AKP as the legitimate political actor'. This enabled the AKP to bring together business, urban poor and conservative religious electoral constituencies. [39]

Conservative democracy has defined the expression of the AKP's will to internalize international norms. Having accepted human rights, democracy and the rule of law as universal values the AKP embraced dominant western values while remaining committed to conservative Islamic roots. The AKP has realized that an anti-western Islamist group would not have the opportunity to continue to hold political power in Turkey. Therefore a pro European foreign policy is seen as the instrument of legitimization for the party not only in the eyes of the Turkish state elite but also in the eyes of the international system. During its term in government the AKP has introduced significant political and economic reforms to consolidate Turkish democracy on the Copenhagen Criteria.[40] Despite difficulties in the process of integration, the AKP has taken steps to ensure the implementation of reforms in line with European standards. In a number of instances these reforms address issues related to the core elements of Turkey's political structures and dynamics. These include reducing the influence of the military in politics, eradicating the death penalty, abolishing the State Security Courts, strengthening gender equality, broadening the freedom of the press, aligning the judiciary with European standards and establishing the supremacy of international agreements in the area of fundamental freedoms over internal legislation.[41]

Ihsan Dagi for instance refers to the AKP as a post-Islamist party which maintains its Islamic credentials on social issues but abandons

Islam as a political programme.[42] Also because of its pro western, liberal democratic orientation, it is argued that the AKP cannot be called Islamist, rather it represents a new articulation of coexistence between Islam and the West which is historically unique. The Islamists view democratization as their first priority believing that it can provide legal cover and legitimacy for their political existence, guarantee basic religious rights and promote social and political networking. Ironically this allows the Islamists to couch their opposition to the Kemalist power apparatus in secular terms. The opportunity cost of this alliance is that Islamists can no longer think in terms of an Islamic state. What Dagi calls post-Islamism has also been defined as the shift from a 'politics of identity to the politics of services'. The AKP in keeping with global developments that favour neo-liberal economic and political values has proven to be a party of service rather than a party of identity. Its emphasis on what it is not for, i.e, Islamic identity, and its appeal to secular rationale rather than religious justifications for its policies, is used to indicate that it is not an Islamic party. The AKP adopted a posture of compromise, used secular political jargon, accepted religious visibility only in individual and social realms, and declared the headscarf issue of minor importance. The Party representatives did not problematize the exclusion of their spouses from official ceremonies (because of their headscarfs) have worked coherently with the IMF and despite sporadic ups and downs continued the strategic alliance with US and Israel. The debate within the state, however, is far from being resolved. The AKP argues that religion belongs to the personal sphere but it can be incorporated into the public and political spheres without compromising the secular state system. Kemalists continue to argue that the secular nature of the state is not safe in the hands of individuals in whose lives religion plays an important role. The determination of the boundaries of the public and the private has therefore emerged as a major area of dispute.[43]

The AKP's approach is indicative of the fact that there are many diverse currents within the Islamic movement in Turkey today. It has been argued that the AKP defends a distinct interpretation of secularism that differs from that of the Kemalist establishment. The debate between the

Kemalists and the AKP is not simply a conflict between secularism and Islamism but rather a discussion about the true meaning and practice of secularism itself. Apart from marginal groups there is overall consensus on secularism in Turkey. The real debate occurs between supporters of different interpretations of secularism. [44] According to Ahmet Kuru a difference has to be recognized between laicism (lack of religious control in legal and judicial processes) and secularism (official neutrality towards religion). Here he argues that a useful category to analyze state-religion relations in Turkey is through the typology of passive and active secularism. The Turkish state originally tended towards assertive secularism and still pursues policies based on that. Yet, there has been debate between supporters of both. The debate will continue since it depends on the incompatibility between assertive secularist state practices and the high religiosity of the Turkish society. This typology also brings into focus the distinction between the image and practices of the Turkish state. The perceived image of the Turkish state has been of a monolithic organization isolated from the fragmentation of society. Yet, analysis shows the fragmentation of state actors in Turkey particularly on the issue of secularism. The depiction of Turkish politics, particularly in the 1990's, as divided between secular forces (the military) and Islamist politicians is no longer valid. The AKP, for instance, defends an alternative mode of secularism in its policies. There is therefore need to understand various interpretations of secularism in order to come to a correct understanding the 'secular' in contemporary Turkish politics.

Conclusions

It has been argued that secularism in Turkey orientalized Turkish society in order to westernize it simply because the westernization of society required its redefinition as oriental in the first place.[45] While the secular aspect of the modernization project has been subject to redefinition its power dimension has not been open to participation and public debate. Under the 'coup' administration in the early 1980's the 'secular' state integrated Islam into its official discourse and permitted some public manifestation of it in order to protect the national community from the leftist 'threat'. In the 1990's however, as part of a larger project of reconfiguring politics from top down, official secularism associated religious practices beyond the confines of individual conscience with reactionism. These re-definitions were not made through public debate and discussion. They were made by extra-political actors of the secular establishment led by the military and through extra-political methods. More importantly, since different definitions of secularism have always involved the promotion of an official Islam, secularism has acted as the catalyst for drawing the lines of demarcation between tolerable and intolerable religious practices. By virtue of promoting an official religion, even when it is confined to individual conscience Turkish secularism did not point to the individualization of religion but to the potential politicization of personal beliefs and thus the blurring of the distinction between the public and the private. In this understanding alternative practices of religion like headscarf wearing are considered political manifestations of a political idea. Hence, Turkish Courts tend to define headscarf wearing not only as defiance against the secular regime but also as an intrusion into other secular lifestyles. This is particularly true of public figures, who are expected to demonstrate their 'secularity' in public and private spheres. These unintended consequences of the Turkish experience have meant that its ability to serve as a model for the Middle East has been limited. As new political landscapes emerge in the Middle East, debates on the Turkish experience also assumes various forms ranging from those that point to its fragility to others who focus on its advantages.[46] Here, the ability of the present government to reconcile conservative values with modern politics and a credible transition to more inclusive governance will be definitive.

Notes

1. From Ihsan Dagi, "The Future of Kemalism and the Istanbul Biennial" in *Turkey Between Democracy and Militarism, Post Kemalist Perspectives,* (Ankara: Orion Publications, 2008). Dagi is faculty at the Middle East Technical University, Ankara
2. Menderes Cinar, "The Justice and Development Party and the Kemalist establishment", in Umit Cizre (ed) *Secular and Islamic Politics in Turkey, The Making of the Justice and Development Party*, (London and New York: Routledge, 2008).

3. Sinan Ciddi, *Kemalism in Turkish Politics, The Republican People's Party, secularism and nationalism,* (London and New York: Routledge, 2009).
4. Pelin Ayan, "Authoritarian Party Structures in Turkey: A Comparison of the Republican People's Party and the Justice and Development Party", *Turkish Studies,* Vol 11, No 2, June 2010.
5. Ciddi, *Kemalism in Turkish Politics.*
6. Cited from Feroz Ahmad, *The Making of Modern Turkey,* (London and New York: Routledge, 1993).
7. J. Habermas, "Modernity versus Postmodernity". *New German Critique,* No 22,1981.
8. Ciddi, *Kemalism in Turkish Politics.*
9. Ciddi, *Kemalism in Turkish Politics.*
10. Bernard Lewis, *The Emergence of Modern Turkey,* (London: Oxford University Press, 1968).
11. Cited from Gerassimos Karabelias, "The Military Institution, Ataturk's Principles and Turkey's Sisyphean Quest for Democracy", *Middle Eastern Studies,* Vol 45, No 1, January 2009.
12. Kemal Karpat, *Turkey's Politics: The Transition to Multiparty System,* (Princeton, NJ: Princeton University Press, 1959).
13. Nicholas Birch, "Turkey: Educational reforms reflect Changing balance of Power in Ankara" *Eurasia Insight*, August 18, 2009.
14. Cited from Ahmad, *The Making of Modern Turkey.*
15. Sibel Bozdogan and Resat Kasaba, *Rethinking Modernity and National Identity in Turkey,* (Seattle: University of Washington Press, 1997).
16. Ziya Onis, "Turkish Modernization and Challenges for the New Europe" home.ku.edu.tr/zonis/Modernization.pdf
17. Idris Bal, *Turkey's Relations With the West and Turkic Republics, The Rise and Fall of the Turkish Model*, (Burlington; Ashgate, 2000).
18. Bal, *Turkey's Relations With the West and Turkic Republics, The Rise and Fall of the Turkish Model*,
19. Menderes Cinar and Burhanettin Duran, "The specific evolution of contemporary Political Islam in Turkey and its 'difference'.", in Umit Cizre (ed) *Secular and Islamic Politics In Turkey, The making of the Justice and Development Party,* (Abingdon, Oxon: Routledge, 2008).
20. M.H. Yavuz, "Is there a Turkish Islam? The Emergence of Convergence and Consensus", *Journal of Muslim Minority Affairs,* Vol 24, No 2, 2004.
21. Cinar and Duran, "The specific evolution of contemporary Political Islam in Turkey and its 'difference".
22. S Zubaida, "Islam and Nationalism: Continuities and Contradictions", *Nations and Nationalism,* 10, 2004.

23. In June 1997, the army removed the Islamist Welfare Party led coalition government with the threat of a military takeover. Without direct military intervention President Suleyman Demirel passed on power to Mesut Yilmaz of ANAP, who formed a minority government in coalition with Bulent Ecevit's Democratic Left Party and with outside support of the CHP. This is referred to as the 28 February process after the military presented an ultimatum to the Erbakan led coalition government at the National Security Council on 28 February 1997. On that day the NSC introduced a bill comprising of 18 specific measures to curb Islamic reactionism and criticized the anti-secular atmosphere in Turkey. It asked the Refah government to take measures to stop the proliferation of Islamist cadres in the bureaucracy and gave a series of press briefings in which religious fundamentalism was declared as the most dangerous enemy facing Turkey.
24. Burhanettin Duran, "Islamist redefinition(s) of European and Islamic identities in Turkey", in Mehmet Ugur and Nergis Canefe (eds) *Turkey and European Integration Accession prospects and issues,* (Abingdon, Oxon: Routledge, 2004).
25. I Sunar and B Toprak, "Islam in Politics: The Case of Turkey", *Government and Opposition*, 18, 1983 cited from Cinar and Duran, "The specific evolution of contemporary Political Islam in Turkey and its 'difference".
26. For details see Cinar and Duran, "The specific evolution of contemporary Political Islam in Turkey and its 'difference".
27. Cinar and Duran, "The specific evolution of contemporary Political Islam in Turkey and its 'difference".
28. U Cizre-Sakallioglu, "Parameters and Strategies of Islam-State Interactions in Republican Turkey", *International Journal of Middle East Studies,* 28, 1996.
29. Soner Cagaptay, "Islam, Secularism and Nationalism in Modern Turkey, Who is a Turk?" (Abingdon, Oxon: Routledge, 2006).
30. Mustafa Erdogan, "Islam in Turkish Politics: Turkey's Quest for Democracy without Islam", *Middle East Critique,* No 15, Fall 1999.
31. A number of parties of the National Outlook Movement have over the years been closed down either by the Constitutional Court or the military. For details see Ahmet Yildiz, "Problematizing the intellectual and political vestiges, From 'welfare' to 'justice and development", in Cizre (ed) *Secular and Islamic Politics In Turkey.*
32. Cinar and Duran, "The specific evolution of contemporary Political Islam in Turkey and its 'difference".
33. U Cizre and M Cinar, "Turkey 2002: Kemalism, Islamism and Politics in the light of the February 28 Process" *South Asia Quarterly,* No 102, 2003.
34. Cited from Cinar and Duran, "The specific evolution of contemporary Political Islam in Turkey and its 'difference".
35. Yildiz, "Problematizing the intellectual and political vestiges".
36. M.K.Kaya, "The AKP Asserts its Conservative Core with Cabinet Reshuffle",

Turkey Analyst, Vol 2, No 9, May 8, 2009 http://www.silkroadstudies.org/new/inside/turkey/2009/090508B.html

37. Yildiz, "Problematizing the intellectual and political vestiges".
38. The AKP developed its normative framework through its official publication, *Conservative Democracy*. The book defines the AKP's conservatism as a ideology that stresses common sense, prudence, and gradual change. It rejects rationalist utopias, Jacobinism and social engineering. At a conference organized to elaborate on the Party's conservative and democratic stand, Erdogan emphasized that the AKP's understanding of conservatism did not mean the conservation of established institutions and relations but implied the protection of important values and principles while pursuing progress. The attempt was to synthesize local and universal values, tradition and modernity and morality and religion. For details see Ahmet Kuru, "From Islamism to Conservative Democracy: The Justice and Development Party in Turkey", Paper presented at the annual meeting of the American Political Science Association, Marriot, Loews, Philadelphia and the Pennsylvania Convention Centre, Philadelphia, PA, August 31, 2006, http://www.allacademic.com/meta/p151181_index.html
39. I. D. Dagi, "The Justice and Development Party: Identity, Politics and Human Rights Discourse in the Search for Security and Legitimacy", in M.H. Yavuz (ed) *The Emergence of a New Turkey: Democracy and the AK Party,* (Salt Lake City: The University of Utah Press, 2006).
40. The EU's Copenhagen Criteria requires stability of institutions guaranteeing democratic governance, human rights and a functioning market economy.
41. Burhanettin Duran, "The Justice and Development Party's new politics'; Steering towards conservative democracy, a revised Islamic agenda or management of new crisis?" in Cizre (ed) *Secular and Islamic Politics In Turkey, The making of the Justice and Development Party.*
42. I.D. Dagi, "Transformation of Islamic Political Identity in Turkey: Rethinking the West and Westernization" *Turkish Studies,* Vol 6, 2005.
43. Jenny B. White, "The End of Islamism? Turkey's Muslim hood Model", in Robert Hefner (ed) *Modern Muslim Politics*, (Princeton University Press, 2005).
44. Kuru, "From Islamism to Conservative Democracy: The Justice and Development Party in Turkey".
45. Cinar, "The Justice and Development Party and the Kemalist establishment".
46. See for instance, Ziya Onis, "Turkey and the Arab Spring: Between Ethics and Self Interest", *Insight Turkey*, Vol 14, No 3, 2012.

8. Islam, Saudi Arabia and the Question of Sovereignty

Md Muddassir Quamar

Introduction

When it comes to Islam and the question of sovereignty, Saudi Arabia offers an interesting example. In the last few decades, like many other Muslim societies, Saudi Arabia has faced the dilemma between tradition and modernity. Islam's predicament with modernity started with exposure to European enlightenment and subsequent technological advancement. The progress made by Europe through rationalising philosophical questions compelled Islamic scholars to come to terms with rationality and efforts were made in the nineteenth century to bridge the gap between Islam and modernity. Islamic Modernism, as it is known, provides a tool to understand this process of change. In the context of the dilemma for popular sovereignty in the Middle East and the question of change occurring in Muslim societies, Islamic Modernism can be employed to look at the Saudi example. Saudi Arabia, an Islamic monarchy, subscribes to the concept that the sovereignty lies with Allah, Quran is the constitution and the power lies with the ruler who is Allah's representative on earth. However, over a period, the monarchy has made numerous systemic adjustments based on the changing socio-political and economic realities. In the process an absolute monarchy has been transformed into a modernising state. The paper tries to find the linkages between the idea of sovereignty in Islam, changes taking place in Saudi society and the demand for political participation in the wake of the Arab Spring. It concludes that Saudi Arabia is slowly evolving into a modernised Islamic state that has the ability to absorb socio-political churning.

Islam and Sovereignty

The Kingdom of Saudi Arabia was established on the basis of Islamic principles as interpreted by Muhammad bin Abdul Wahhab.[1] The religious reformer emphasised on the need for establishment of a state on the basis of the principles of *tawheed*. The idea of *tawheed*, according to Islam, is the most important aspect of an individual's faith. Quranic and prophetic teachings put immense emphasis on the sovereignty of Allah (*tawheed*) over the entire universe and all its beings without any exception. This emphasis on *tawheed* for the faithful, however, did not talk about location of sovereignty within state structures as was the case in modernising Europe. The modern concept is defined as locating a political body that possesses ultimate, final and independent authority, whose decisions are binding upon all citizens, groups and institutions in the state. It is from this concept of absolute authority that the idea of popular sovereignty as propounded by Rousseau came into force in the eighteenth century and changed the state structures and the citizens or the people became the sovereign.

The Islamic principles based in faith did not undergo any major change since they took root in the seventh century. It followed and built upon the philosophy of monotheism that predated Islam and established that absolute authority lies with Allah. The idea did not face any major challenge within the Islamic world; though numerous interpretations and understanding of the concept of *tawheed* existed. Moreover, Muslim societies for most of Islam's history prior to modernity were ruled by empires and dynasties. Islamic states ruled on the basis that Allah is sovereign and the ruler – be it Caliph, King, Imam or Sultan – is the representative of Allah on earth and has to rule according to the divine laws as established by the Prophet and spread by his followers. Thus the concept of rule on the basis of *shari'a* comes into the picture.

The problem started when the Muslim world encountered a modernised Europe that led to a variety of reactions. The Ottoman Empire started a number of reformatory steps to come to terms with modern Europe, however, the Caliphate succumbed to internal and external pressures in early twentieth century. Moreover, the colonial dominance of European power led to varied reactions from numerous Muslim thinkers and reformers to the ideas of modern state system. Religious scholars, such as, Abul Ala' Maududi in the Indian subcontinent, Syed Qutb in Egypt, Ayatollah Khomeini and Ali Shariati in Iran argued that the basic distinction between the Western and Islamic political systems is that the former places authority in either the state or in the people through the notion of popular sovereignty while the latter puts absolute authority in God. The argument was placed to say that the solution to the problems confronting Muslim societies can be found only in Islam through going back to its roots.

But there were other set of scholars, such as Muhammad Abduh, Syed Ahmad Khan and Ayatollah Naini, who reacted differently and argued about rationalising the Islamic principles and concepts in the light of Western modernity. Islamic Modernism, as it came to be known, 'endeavoured to devise a model for reorganizing the structure of authority, for providing a foundation to build a new society, and for drawing the basic principle of rule making' as a solution to the problems confronting Muslim world.[2] However, these societies are still struggling with the problem of state and governance and have not been able to find a balance between the faith, modernity and providing a political system that can effectively respond to the needs of its citizens. It has been highlighted by the protests movements in the Arab world, popularly referred to as 'Arab Spring'.

The problem of finding a balance between Islam and modernity was faced by the newer political entities that emerged in the Muslim world in the early twentieth century. Emerging from or as an effect of the dismemberment of the Ottoman Empire and the end of colonialism, these states adopted a variety of systems to govern the people in order to come to terms with challenges facing them. When it comes to Saudi Arabia, the process of modernisation embarked upon by the monarchy, does not fits in either with the liberal democratic ideals nor can it be completely rationalised on the basis of traditional Islamic notions of state. Thus employing an Islamic modernist perspective to understand these changes may provide better insights. But before taking up the Saudi case, one needs to look at the variety of political systems that different Muslim states evolved to deal with the problems posed by modernity.

Evolution of Modern States in the Muslim World

Large parts of the Arab-Muslim world were under Ottoman domination till its disintegration in the early twentieth century. It led to some parts of the region coming under European colonial domination while others carved out independent states with or without colonial influence. However, most of these countries became independent with the end of the Second World War. The geographic boundaries which defined states in the region after the disintegration of the Ottoman Empire and end of European colonialism were non-existent before and were mainly the products of colonialism. Thus a number of states that were formed in the region were artificial creations of understanding between the colonial powers and the local elites, especially in the Levant, the Arab Gulf and North Africa. Though there are exceptions, such as, Turkey, Egypt, Iran and Saudi Arabia, that either had historical legacy or were a product of effort by local rulers. But these states – be it Syria, Iraq, Jordan, Egypt, Turkey, Iran, Saudi Arabia and others – embarked on different journeys in the evolution of their political system.

Turkey, the seat of Ottoman Empire, embarked on a secular-nationalist polity under Mustafa Kamal Ataturk, with greater military domination. The Turkish military appointed itself as the guardian of the infant nation-state. Turkey has slowly evolved into an Islamist dominated Western style democracy, with diminishing role for military in politics. The Turkish experiment has proved to be one of the most successful efforts at a Muslim state with popular sovereignty, a secular constitution and a religious-nationalist identity.[3] This is not to argue that the journey for Turkey was smooth. Iran, on the other hand, had seen a constitutional movement as early as in the first decade of the twentieth century. It remained under the rule of a monarchy till the 1979 Islamic revolution. Iran, thus, became an Islamic republic with a religious constitution and greater role for the clergy in the state. The Islamic republic of Iran, though, has been successful in creating a state with a religious-nationalist identity and a working system of participatory politics.[4]

The political systems in the Arab states that emerged from the ruins of the empire or out of colonial legacy can be broadly categorised as either monarchical such as Saudi Arabia, Jordan and Morocco or military dominated republics like Egypt, Iraq and Syria. But every state developed a different mechanism and acquired a different shape as far as their political systems were concerned. Egypt, for example, became independent in 1922 and remained under a monarchy with a popularly elected government. The continuous and increasing intervention of the king under colonial influence led to intensification of the nationalist movement. A military *coup d'état* in 1952 resulted in the abolition of the monarchy and declaration of the Egyptian republic under a group of nationalist military officers. However, it gradually, degenerated into a dictatorial military regime. The large-scale participation of youth in the protests that forced the exit of Hosni Mubarak in February 2011, was seen as a product of failure of the military led republican form of government. Subsequently, however, a popularly elected Islamist government abortively struggled to take the republic forward in a direction that is responsive, stable and Islamic at the same time.

Syria, another important country in the region started as a republican state after its independence, unlike Egypt, but soon came under a military-led Ba'athist government that transformed into family-dictatorship and is now struggling with the effects of Arab Spring. Iraq, Yemen, Libya, Algeria, Tunisia, all of which became republican struggled to find a political system that can balance between the religious and nationalist identity without embarking upon dictatorship.

If the republics could not find stable systems that can absorb political aspirations of the people and respond to their socio-economic hopes, the monarchies could not do well either. The only difference was that they provided stable governments but remained brutally forceful in dealing with any dissent and in coercing political aspirations. They sustained their rule through a mixture of tribal loyalty, distribution of wealth, and modernisation effort through top-to-bottom reforms. However, this did not mean that they did not have to struggle with the wave of Arab Spring protests. Morocco, Jordan, Bahrain, Oman, United Arab Emirates, Kuwait, Qatar as well as Saudi Arabia have struggled to come to terms with the demand for popular political participation and a share in the decision making process though the degree and intensity of demands varied.

The Monarchy and its People

In 1902, Abdulaziz bin Abdulrahman Al-Saud (Ibn Saud), embarked on a military mission to regain the family rule and benefitted from the changing political landscape in the region to gain authority over large parts of the Arabian Peninsula by 1925. The monarchy consolidated power and gained legitimacy under the founder king through a mixture of Islam, tribal loyalty, co-option and coercion. He was aware of the need to develop powerful external alliance for consolidation of the state, thus built strong ties with the British and later with the US. The most important aspect of the monarchy, however, was proclamation of Allah's sovereignty (*tawheed*) in the holy lands. It was legitimised with the help of the aligned *ulema* of the Wahhabi school.

The formation of a kingdom in the name of establishing sovereignty of Allah, in a region with high importance accorded to faith, provided an impeccable tool to remain unchallenged as far as the ruler's legitimacy was concerned. The discovery of oil and the riches it generated provided another tool to the Saudi monarchy in enhancing its legitimacy through distribution of wealth. Thus the monarchy and the people established a 'social-contract' that provided absolute authority to the ruler.[5] It was an arrangement where the people did not have any role in the political system either in practical terms or theoretically. But the people had a stake in the economic development and modernisation. However, this did not mean that the monarchy did not face challenges to its legitimacy and authority. Individuals and groups from within and outside have posed challenge to the political system from time to time. They were mainly not against the theoretical basis on which the kingdom was established; rather they questioned the way Allah's sovereignty was being implemented.

The only effective challenge posed to the theoretical basis of Saudi state was in the 1960s during the hey-days of Pan-Arabism. It was the time when Egypt, under the leadership of Gamal Abdul Nasser, launched severe ideological attacks on Arab monarchies, which were thought to be the puppets of Western imperialism. Influcnccd by it, some movement were built up in the kingdom as a large number of Egyptian nationals were employed in Saudi Arabia. The 'Free Princes' movement led by Prince Talal called for abolishment of the monarchy and proclamation of a republic with a written constitution.[6] The 'Free Princes' were given refuge in Egypt from where they launched attacks on Saudi monarchy. The rivalry worsened when Saudi Arabia and Egypt entered into a proxy-war in North Yemen backing the royal family and the republicans respectively. The situation, however, changed with the formation of Yemen Arab Republic and changing geo-political circumstances, particularly due to the devastating Arab defeat in the 1967 war. It was a major challenge for Saudi Arabia that questioned the core of the state structure. The idea that sovereignty shall lie with the people was a direct challenge for the monarchy as through such means its power and authority came under direct threat.

Another major challenge that the monarchy faced was in the wake of 1979 Islamic revolution in Iran. The abolition of a monarchy in the neighbourhood and Khomeini's rhetoric for export of the revolution was seen as threatening by the Saudi monarchy, particularly with sizeable Shi'i population in its Eastern Province. The fear was not unfounded because the province – where most of the oil-fields are located – witnessed numerous incidents of rioting and anti-government demonstrations. The monarchy used its military to curb the protests. As if this was not enough, on 20 November 1979, the incident of seizure of Kaaba happened. A group of zealous Islamists, led by Juhaiman al-Uthaibi, took over the mosque in Mecca during annual Hajj pilgrimage and declared the arrival of Mahdi[7], and demanded that people follow them, as according to them the monarchy had become corrupted and anti-Islamic.[8] The monarchy regained control of the Mosque with the help of French paratroopers. It responded to the incident with increased emphasis on religion in public life and greater role for *ulema* in the government. Though this was a major challenge, it did not question the theoretical aspect of the monarchical government but casted aspersions on the functional aspect of Islamic principles.

Saudi Arabia's ability to withstand a crisis was again put to test in the aftermath of the 1990-91 Gulf war. Iraqi invasion and annexation of Kuwait and the US-led Operation Desert Storm for Kuwaiti liberation was followed with the rise of domestic discontent in the Gulf Cooperation Council (GCC) states. Several groups, both liberals and conservatives, petitioned the Saudi monarchy to start political reforms. Though the demand for opening up the political system for the people was building up in the kingdom from earlier, it gained momentum in the aftermath of the Kuwait crisis in the form of the petition movement.[9] The monarchy responded with a series of reform measures indicating its willingness to accommodate the demands of the people. On 1 March 1992, King Fahd issued the Basic System of Governance that re-emphasised on the Islamic ideals of the state. Likewise, the statutes for governing the *Majlis al-Shura* (Consultative Council) and the Law of the Provinces were issued. These were substantial reform measures by Saudi standard. Though the state had a tradition of consultation and taking varied opinions into account in the matters of state, this was institutionalised for the first time.

In the aftermath of the Kuwait crisis, the decision to allow stationing of foreign 'infidel' forces inside the kingdom, led to spread of extremist ideas. It was a time when greater demands for political reforms echoed in the kingdom from various spectrums of political leanings. The religious groups, such as, Committee for Defense of Legitimate Rights (CDLR) called for more reforms but were rebuked by the monarchy, it was compelled to disband and its leaders arrested. However, there were more radical groups that openly called for overthrow of the monarchy as, according to them, it had lost its Islamic legitimacy. The most prominent was the al-Qaeda, led by Osama bin Laden, who fled first to Sudan and then to Afghanistan, after the monarchy revoked his citizenship and issued orders to arrest him. The group was allegedly involved in the 1996 Khobar bombings, which killed 19 American citizens. The intensity of the problem, however, was recognised only after the 9/11 attacks in the

US and the 2003 Riyadh bombings.

The monarchy, now, recognised the gravity of the problem. It had already started a series of reform measures in the early 1990s. But the demand for political opening did not abate. The people through petitions, and sometimes through the use of media, and civil society started to voice their concern about the problems facing the state and demanded a role in the decision making process. The monarchy initiated legal, political and social reforms to respond to the people's demands. Building upon the earlier reform measures numerous steps were taken to make the judiciary more responsive to people's problems. In 2005, the monarchy introduced elections for choosing half of the municipal council members.[10] It was a first of its kind step in Saudi Arabia and was, indeed, an important reform measure towards political participation by Saudi standards.

Furthermore, educational reform measures were introduced to improve the quality and access of education for the entire population including that of women. The monarchy allowed functioning of a civil society and voluntary sector. Steps, such as, the national dialogue and interfaith dialogue, were taken to encourage debate on various aspects of life in Saudi Arabia. Furthermore, measures were taken to diversify the economy and localisation of the job market to deal with the rising problem of unemployment and increasing population of youth.[11]

The challenges that Saudi Arabia faced in the aftermath of the Kuwait crisis and the 9/11 attacks were multifaceted and significant. Although the theoretical basis of the Islamic monarchy, namely the concept of Allah's sovereignty, was not under contest, the voices mainly questioned the practical aspect of the functioning of the state. The Islamists were demanding greater role for religion in governance, education, foreign policy and other aspects of life as they believed that the monarchy has compromised with the tenets of *shari'a*. On the other hand, the liberals were cautious in not asking for abolishment of the monarchy and establishment of a republic. Rather the liberal impulse was to demand for political participation and greater freedom and rights in public life. The monarchy responded with substantial reform measures to satisfy the demands of an increasingly educated middle-class. The after-effects of

Arab Spring in the kingdom and the debate on popular sovereignty have to be seen in the context of earlier demands for reform and the response from the monarchy.

Arab Spring and its After-effects

Once the protests started in Tunisia in December 2010 and spread to Egypt and other parts of the Arab world, the gullibility of the state structures became increasingly clear. The people, who had expected to have a political system that is responsive to their demands and provides space for participation in the decision making process, were not satisfied with the state of affairs. The state not just failed in providing economic development and social progress but allowed a limited opening in the politics. The *Arab Human Development Report 2004* had highlighted the deficit in political freedom and good governance and had argued that a more responsive and broad-based political structure is imminent if the Arab states had to embark on human development.[12] The Arab Spring, in a way, was a popular representation of a demand for good governance. As protests started in Bahrain, other Gulf states recognised the magnitude of the problem. The Kingdom of Saudi Arabia witnessed a number of events indicating towards popular demand for political opening and reforms.

The most important aspect was that, even though, Saudi Arabia earlier faced demands for reform but it had not acquired manifestation of popular protests. Thus the situation emerging from the Arab Spring was intriguing for the monarchy. More importantly, the political, social and economic condition of Saudi Arabia was not very different from the countries that were facing large-scale protests. Like other countries, the oil-rich kingdom faced problems, such as, increasing youth population, unemployment, accusations of corruption and amassing of wealth by the members of the ruling family, a changing society and an increasing population that aspired for greater freedom and political participation.[13] Moreover, allegations of discrimination against Shi'is and lack of effective steps to fulfil the demand for greater freedom for women in public life became starker in the wake of the Arab Spring. The monarchy devised a strategy with a combination of political, economic and military measures to deal with the challenge.

The political moves were taken to give an impression that the state was serious about bringing reforms and to discourage protests by invoking religion. In February 2011, the Grand Mufti declared protests against the rulers as 'un-Islamic', while in October 2011 Abdul Rahman Al-Sudais, Imam of Kaaba, in his Friday sermon during Hajj, appealed to the Muslims to "avoid course of collision" and asked the leaders of Islamic countries to "fulfil their duty of maintaining security and stability ...".[14] The invocation of religion and faith to deal with the problem was mainly an assertion that the state structure and its theoretical basis will not be compromised. Thus making it clear, at the outset, that any demand for reform can be accepted on the functional aspect of the state and the system can be strengthened but no change will be made in the theoretical basis of the state. It was a posture to emphasise that the power and authority of the monarchy will not be diluted.

Politically, the most important task at hand was to respond to the restive Shi'i population. The Shi'is of Saudi Arabia have traditionally felt marginalised and have unsuccessfully demanded better educational and employment opportunities.[15] The ruling family did not want to take any chance with the Eastern Province, which has a history of Shi'i unrest. King Abdullah had been accommodative of the concerns of the Shi'i population and had taken steps to instil confidence among them. For example, in April 2003 Abdullah received a petition called 'Partners in One Nation' from a Shi'i delegation.[16] The National Dialogue started in 2003 and the interfaith dialogue conference in 2008 were initiatives in the same direction. But the monarchy used force to keep the situation under control in the wake of the Arab Spring.

In addition to the unrest among Shi'is, the impact of Arab Spring in Saudi Arabia manifested in the movement for women's right to drive. The demand, though not new, gained momentum in May-June 2011 after Manal al-Sharif, a Saudi women's rights activist, posted a video of herself driving a car on YouTube. She was arrested but was pardoned by the king. In another incident, in September 2011, the king pardoned a woman who was sentenced to 10 lashes by a court for driving. Such moves were taken to show the readiness of the monarchy to be accommodative of aspirations of youth, men and women. Saudi Arabia has for long faced criticism for lack of freedom and rights for women. Gender segregation is a norm and *hijab* for women in public life is enforced by law. Though education has led to some opening, a section of religious leaders continue to oppose any public role for women. In September 2011, before the municipal elections, King Abdullah announced that women would be allowed to vote and contest in 2015 municipal elections. Furthermore, it was announced that women would be nominated in the *Majlis al-Shoura* (Shoura Council). In line with this commitment, on 16 January 2013, the king nominated 20 women, including a Shi'i, to the 150-member *Majlis al-Shoura*. It was a move to send a strong message to the masses showing willingness on the part of the Saudi ruler to deal with the issue of demands for women's rights.

Moreover, Saudi Arabia announced a slew of economic benefits for the masses to complement the politico-religious moves. In February 2011, King Abdullah announced a financial package worth US$37 billion and this was followed by another package on 16 March 2011 to the tune of US$130 billion. It was declared that the unemployment benefit would be increased to US$500 per month and minimum salary to US$750 per month and all public servants would receive a bonus that equalled their two months' salary. The monarchy announced 500,000 new homes for the poor will be built. In addition, it was announced that all students would receive a bonus equalling their two months' education allowance with the March 2011 package. Measures were taken to show the readiness of the state to provide access to quality education to all the citizens. For example, the King Abdullah Foreign Scholarship Programme was extended for third term. The flagship programme which supports Saudi students to go abroad for higher education would now continue till 2020.[17] Moreover, the budgetary allocation for social welfare witnessed sharp increase during 2011-2013 to avoid any chances of repercussion due to lack of economic benefit.[18]

Furthermore, Saudi Arabia, took a number of security measures to pre-empt protests as an expression of strength of the state. Immediately after the call for organisation of the 'day of rage' on 11 March 2011, police and military personals were deployed all over the country. Special Forces were positioned in sensitive areas, particularly in the Eastern Province and Najran. The security in Riyadh, Jeddah and other important cities were enhanced. In the meanwhile King Abdullah, who was convalescing in Morocco after a surgery in the US for undisclosed ailment, returned to Saudi Arabia on 23 February 2011. The Ministry of Interior prohibited public protests and demonstrations. A number of political activists who had apparently voiced their concerns over the treatment of Shi'is were detained and put in prison. On 11 March, Riyadh was turned into a military camp with security forces camping all over the city while the people preferred to remain inside their homes.[19] Barring a few incidents in Qatif and Hofuf, where the security personal rounded up some people who had allegedly collected to protest, the kingdom did not witness protests.

These measures, however, did not deter everyone into submission. Though, the enhanced security prevented large-scale protests, smaller protests and clashes between Shi'i demonstrators and security forces were reported throughout the 2011 and 2012. Historically, coercion has played an important role in providing stability to the state and any dissent is taken as a security risk by the monarchy. In his address to the nation on 17 March 2011, the king took a hard-line view towards the calls for protests and warned the people against possible unrest. Praising the security forces he remarked: "threats to the nation's security and stability will not be tolerated."[20] Later, in July 2011, a new anti-terror law was introduced which many analysts termed would serve as a tool to curb genuine political dissent.[21] Though the situation remained by and peaceful, there were reports of protests in cities like Awwamiyah and Qatif.

In October 2012, 19 men were charged with 'instigating chaos and sedition' and 'gathering illegally' and were put in jail in Qassim province. Furthermore, on 9 March 2013, two prominent human rights activists Abdullah al-Hamid and Mohammad al-Qahtani, the co-founders of the

Association of Civil and Political Rights (ACPRA), were sentenced to 10 years jail and the ACPRA was dissolved for violating Saudi laws and giving 'inappropriate information to foreign groups'.[22] With such measures, the monarchy gave a strong message that any dissent would be dealt by force. It has helped in keeping the situation firmly under control and peaceful.

With the help of moves to reflect political desire for administrative and social reforms, invocation of religion to declare protests as against Islam, financial packages and beefed-up security, Saudi Arabia prevented any major trouble in the wake of the Arab Spring. The responses of the state were devised to emphasise that it would not compromise on the theoretical and structural aspects of the state. At the same time, the monarchy wanted to show its readiness to provide political opening for the people. The Saudi stand meant that Allah's sovereignty cannot be questioned though the political system can be made more participatory. An Islamist modernist approach, perhaps, can be located at this juncture, whereby the fundamental principle of the state structure was kept intact but systemic changes are being introduced. Although the concept does not provide any model political system on which the changes in the state and polity of Saudi Arabia can be measured. Nonetheless, despite introducing numerous reform measures, the monarchy has a long way to go as far as becoming a truly representative and participatory political system.

Conclusion

The Saudi state subscribes to Wahhabi interpretation of Islamic principles, which provides legitimacy to its political structure of Allah's sovereignty, implementation of *shari'a* law and power and authority to the ruler as divine representative. However, the hereditary-monarchical political system has been sustained through a mixture of tribal alliances, alignment with dominant religious thought, use of force to deal with dissent, distribution of wealth and introduction of a process of modernisation. It has succeeded in dealing with numerous problems by keeping the religious character intact and introducing reform measures for greater political opening. The political system again faces major challenges in the wake of Arab Spring, but has used its philosophical and material resources to indicate a willingness for allowing political expressions and greater participation in the decision making process. An Islamic modernist approach, which calls for rationalising the Islamic principles in the light of modern thought, can explain the changing socio-political realities in the kingdom. If one looks at the concept of sovereignty in Islam, the changing socio-political environment in Saudi Arabia and the response of the monarchy, it can be argued that the kingdom has embarked on a path of a modernised Islamic state capable of responding to the socio-political demands of its people.

Notes

1. The eighteenth century religious reformer was born in central Arabia, who found an ally in the rulers of Diriyah. This religious-political alliance attempted political unification of the entire peninsula thrice. The earlier two states were dismantled by Ottoman backed rulers and the third military campaign that started in 1902 culminated in the formation of the Kingdom of Saudi Arabia in 1932. For details see, Madawi Al-Rasheed, *History of Saudi Arabia*, (Cambridge: University Press, 2002).
2. Mansoor Moaddel, *Islamic Modernism, Nationalism and Fundamentalism: Episode and Discourse*, (London: The University of Chicago Press, 2005) p. 2.
3. For more see, Muge Ankur (ed.), *Democratic Consolidation in Turkey: State, Political Parties, Civil Society, Civil-Military Relations, Socio-Economic Development, EU, Rise of Political Islam and Separatist Kurdish Nationalism* (Florida: Universal Press, 2012).
4. For more see, Samih K. Farsoun and Mehrdad Mashayekhi (eds.), *Iran: Political Culture in the Islamic Republic* (London: Routledge, 1992).
5. F. Gregory Gause III, *Oil Monarchies: Domestic and Security Challenges in the Arab Gulf States* (New York: Council on Foreign Relations, 1994).
6. See Madawi al-Rasheed, *History of Saudi Arabia.*
7. According to Islamic belief, Mahdi would be send by Allah to redeem the Muslim *Ummah* and will rule the world and rid it of all its evil before the Day of Judgement.
8. For details see, Yaroslav Trofimov, *The Siege of Mecca: the forgotten uprising in Islam's holiest shrine and the birth of al Qaeda*, (New York: Anchor Books, 2008).
9. Richard H. Dekmejian, "The Liberal Impulse In Saudi Arabia", *Middle East*

Journal, 57 (3), Summer 2003, pp. 400-413.

10. Most of the members who were elected had religious leanings, even though, there were a large number of liberal candidates in the fray. The next elections scheduled for 2009 were postponed till 2011. It finally took place on 29 September 2011.
11. For a detailed study on the reforms in various sectors in Saudi Arabia, see; Joseph A. Kèchichian, *Legal and Political Reforms in Saudi Arabia* (London: Routledge, 2013).
12. United Nations Development Programme, *Arab Human Development Report 2004: Towards Freedom in the Arab World* (New York, 2005).
13. For a detailed analysis, see; Leigh Nolan, "Managing Reform?: Saudi Arabia and the King's Dilemma," *Brookings Doha Center*, May 2011.
14. Badea Abu Al-Naja, "Avoid course of collision and Chaos, Makkah imam tells Muslims", *Arab News*, 11 November 2011, http://www.arabnews.com/node/397762.
15. "The Shiite Question in Saudi Arabia", *International Crisis Group*, 19 September 2005, http://www.crisisgroup.org/en/regions/middle-east-north-africa/iraq-iran-gulf/saudi-arabia/045-the-shiite-question-in-saudi-arabia.aspx. See also, Mai Yamani, "Saudi Arabia's Shias Stand Up", *Project Syndicate*, 11 March 2009, http://www.project-syndicate.org/commentary/saudi-arabia-s-shia-stand-up.
16. Richard H. Dekmejian, "The Liberal Impulse in Saudi Arabia", Middle East Journal, 57 (3), Summer 2003, pp. 400-413.
17. Ministry of Higher Education, Kingdom of Saudi Arabia, "Extension of King Abdullah scholarship programme to study abroad for the third term", 11 February 2013, [Arabic] http://www.mohe.gov.sa/ar/news/Pages/news-2-4-1434.aspx.
18. US-Saudi Business Council, "Saudi Arabia's 2013 Budget Continues focus on Investment", available at http://www.us-sabc.org/custom/news/details.cfm?id=1380#.UWMNiqJTCSo.
19. Eman Al Nafjan, "Saudi Arabia's day of little rage", *The Guardian*, 12 March 2011, http://www.guardian.co.uk/commentisfree/2011/mar/12/saudi-protests.
20. "Saudi King warns against unrest while boosting benefits", *BBC News*, 18 March 2011, http://www.bbc.co.uk/news/world-middle-east-12781068.
21. "Proposed Saudi Arabia anti-terror law would strangle peaceful protest", *Amnesty International*, 22 July 2011, http://www.amnesty.org/en/news-and-updates/proposed-saudi-arabian-anti-terror-law-would-strangle-peaceful-protest-2011-07-22.
22. Mohammad al-Ghanim, "order sentencing two founders of human rights association to jail, dissolution of the association.....", *Al-Riyadh, 10* March 2013, [Arabic] http://www.alriyadh.com/2013/03/10/article816175.html.

9. The Shift: *Israel in the 1990s and Beyond*

Priya Singh,

Introduction

Israel is generally portrayed as a small state and is viewed as a society in formation, undergoing continuous construction and crystallization. It is a post-industrial, information society with blurred geo-political and social boundaries. Deemed as a warfare society, it is a deeply divided one. Israel is a democratic, an ideological and a Jewish society. It is an overburdened society whose political system is preoccupied with enduring, substantial difficulties. Many of Israel's problems still remain unresolved. They have accumulated and intensified over the years. The political and social Left formed the nascent Jewish state and society. The Left stood for a separate Jewish society, social-democratic values, new social forms (the Kibbutz, the Moshav, the Histadrut, Youth movements),[1] and a Jewish state in a part of the Land of Israel only, thereby enabling the formation of a separate Palestinian state. However, with time its creativity and popular support were on the wane, and in 1977 it lost power to the Right, which has for the most part dominated politics and policies since then. In addition to the political shift to the Right, Israel has been undergoing other large-scale transformations. Globalisation is another crucial trend, intensifying Israel's integration into the world economic and state system and reshaping the role of the state. The privatisation of state companies and services complement these changes. Liberalisation is another process that has reoriented Israelis to a discourse of and insistence on individual rights and liberties, personal interests, neo-liberal values, and a de-emphasis of social solidarity and cohesion. These processes of change have prompted a further fragmentation of Israeli society.[2]

Hence, Israel is undergoing deep processes of change. Such processes are evident in the physical, cultural, social, political, and economic spheres.[3] From the 1990s, Israel acquired a new profile — one that is remarkably different from that of the previous decades. These profound changes have been caused, or at the least accompanied, by perceptual and attitudinal transformations. Many Israelis are significantly altering the way in which they view themselves, their social status, and their relations with the state. They are adopting new attitudes toward family, neighbourhood, and society, and are modifying their perceptions of how they should carry out their interactions in both the public sphere and in the private domain. More and more Israelis are altering their attitudes towards collective and communal values and commitments. In Israel, there has emerged—along with the growing power of the traditional groupings that display persistence in their commitment to the state and its communitarian heritage—more than just emerging post-materialist, post-modernist and individualistic tendencies and groups. However, in a state where there have always existed deep social, ethnic, ideological, religious cleavages and distinct powerful traditional sub-cultures, there has emerged strong opposition to those new trends and new politics. Thus, simultaneous with the growing support for new forms of pluralism and liberalisation, equally large social segments have preserved their previous parochial, nationalist and traditional religious attitudes.

The emergence of such contradictory and competing social and ideological trends, the persistence of traditional social and political inclinations and the resurgence of traditional religious and nationalist predispositions intensify internal tensions. These make the Israeli society and polity more complex. Furthermore, these tensions and tendencies not only make it a pluralist society with a new approach, but also have a profound effect on the Israeli state, its power, and its ability to firmly control and guide social, political, and economic development.[4] The intent here is to explore the developments that have given birth to certain novel social and political discourses, and to examine their influence on the status, hegemony, and power of the Israeli state. More specifically, the primary goal here is to examine discourses pertaining to the dynamics of sovereignty, citizenship, and loyalty; decline of the state and statism; the cultural divergence and the democracy debates.

The Dynamics of Sovereignty, Citizenship and Allegiance

New ideas concerning the limits of Israel's sovereignty and the nature of citizenship have caused a perceptible reduction in allegiance to the state and its various organizations; consequently, it encounters difficulties in imposing its policies on the citizens and mobilizing them to perform traditional functions.[5] In turn, this weakness further encourages demands of individuals and interest groups on the state concerning rights, entitlements, and the allocation of material resources. There are indications that both society and the state must accept greater pluralism. Yet, because of the strength of various traditional and conservative forces, the road toward a liberal democracy that permits cultural pluralism and active citizenship is expected to be difficult and protracted.

To facilitate an understanding of the changing meaning of citizenship, sovereignty, and allegiance in Israel, a brief outline of the emerging new features of the Israeli social and political environment is necessary. In the social sphere, the most significant developments have not only been the disappearance of the three loose ideological blocs, (labour, civil and religious) but also the gradual bridging of certain old cleavages, on one hand, and an intensification of antagonisms along lines of other divisions, on the other. The processes of enhanced economic and political integration of Sephardi Jews[6] and Israeli Arabs[7] on one hand, and the growing alienation and tension between religious and secular Jews, on the other, are facilitated by the decay of the old ideological blocs, which no longer have the standing to control national resources, retain a firm hold over their members, and prevent major social and political clashes. These contradictory processes have wider social ramifications. There is thus, a pronounced decline in the readiness to become and remain members of established national and communal organizations, such as the government bureaucracy, the IDF (The Israel Defence Forces,) and the Kibbutz and Moshav movements, the Histradut (Organized Labour) and other such collectives. The other significant developments comprise the persistent diminution of the importance of the traditional mass-membership branch parties, such as the Likud and the Labour and the continuous crisis in the Knesset (Parliament), signifying the decline of the legislative branch of the government. Finally, there has been a significant shift in the Israeli economy from firm governmental control and its deep involvement in all aspects of the economy, to a rapidly growing process of liberalisation, deregulation and privatisation. These new features of the social, political and economic spheres constitute the current settings for the public discussion of sovereignty, citizenship and allegiance and ultimately, of the status of the Israeli state.

In Israel, people associate the term state sovereignty mainly with its external dimension, which is closely related, first, to the notion of borders, and second, to the actual application of the state's undertaking to protect the state's borders and everything that is located inside these borders. There is another aspect of a state's sovereignty pertaining to the use by the state's agencies of a number of special rights that are possessed by no other institution within the boundaries of the state. In Israel, the various agencies of the state have limited claim to such rights, as well as limited capabilities to implement them. The term sovereignty per se, its various interpretations, and the multiple arguments concerning its limits, location, division, and the possibility that it is rapidly dwindling, are not frequently debated upon in public political discussions. Nevertheless, as in other western democracies, Israeli citizens and residents face serious questions when encountering its practical implications, on the one hand, and the state agencies face growing difficulties applying it, on the other.[8]

Essentially, there are three types of arguments made by three different groups that are directed against the state's claims of complete sovereignty and hegemony within the territories currently held by Israel. The first challenge is generated by those Israelis, both Palestinians and Jews, who support the Palestinians' demand for self-determination which intentionally or inadvertently may lead to the establishment of an independent state. The second group that seriously criticizes Israel's positions with regard to the Arab Question is an indefinite group of Jewish people termed as the post Zionists.[9] The third group rejecting the state's claim for full sovereignty on an ideational basis is that of the ultra-orthodox Haredi Jews.[10] While the Israeli Palestinians and the Israeli Jews, who support their claims, on the one hand, and the Haredim on the other, are becoming more focused in their arguments against the State's sovereignty, the trend among the secular Jews is toward a different direction totally, that is, toward political apathy and abstention from active political participation.

Unlike the discussion on sovereignty, the discourse of Israeli citizenship is more open and focussed. It is the Israeli Palestinian community along with their Jewish supporters who constitute the most significant source of challenge to the traditional concept of citizenship in Israel and question not only the nature of Israeli-Palestinian citizenship but also the entire question of Israeli citizenship. The basic contention of this group is that Israel has been a Fascist Colonialist state—due to its discriminating attitudes and actions towards the Palestinian community along with the unmitigated appropriation of its lands within the green line. The solution, they argue lies in the creation of a secular democratic state instead of a Jewish state. A somewhat less radical approach within this community is that Israel should become the state of all its citizens. The outcome of these demands has been a growing debate within Israel regarding the possibility/viability of a state of Israel devoid of its Jewish and Zionist characteristics.[11] Besides the Israeli-Palestinian component, the Haredi community also has been a continually assertive and combative opponent of the Israeli notion of citizenship. While enjoying most of the rights granted by the Israeli state, the Haredim are far from accepting and fulfilling a number of duties expected by the Israeli state from its citizens, the most conspicuous example being, refraining from compulsory military service. These groups along with a number of other minority groups significantly add to the visible political and social tensions characteristic of contemporary Israel. [12]

On the one hand, a vast majority of the Jews in Israel declare their loyalty to the state and their readiness to accept its laws and authority though, in view of the current complex patterns of social segmentation, Haredi Jews and various groups of secular post Zionists and Israeli

Palestinians and their supporters continue to demonstrate greater loyalty to their ethnic, ideological and religious communities than to the Jewish state. On the other hand, there can be detected clear and strong tendencies within Israel toward individuation, a new emphasis on the attainment of self-interested goals and growing individual assertiveness. These simultaneous developments have given birth to strong demands for the rights of both individual and group self-determination, social and political recognition, acceptance of their associations, access to policy-making and policy makers, and a fairer share of national resources.

Generally speaking, it appears that instead of a great degree of patriotism and full loyalty to their state, a sizeable number of Israelis are adopting divided or even ambiguous loyalties toward the state. Apparently more Israelis are groping with the difficult questions of whether and to what extent individualism, self-determination, and self-fulfilment can coexist with patriotism, loyalty and commitment to the state, and the accomplishment of its goals.

Decline of the State and Statism

This segment focuses on the state's role in the economy and the consequences of its actions on the extent of its power.[13] In the last decade Israel has been experiencing what can be termed as revolutionary/radical changes in its politico-economic landscape. What appeared to have been some of the country's most firmly entrenched institutions, (the Histradut, the Kibbutz movement etc.) many of them dating back to the Yishuv (pre-state) days, were seen to be crumbling. Along with these spectacular occurrences, a series of less dramatic developments were also taking place, the consequence of which on the Israeli economic scene might be of much greater significance. These processes affected the set of institutional, administrative and legal arrangements under which individual economic agents operate, and which constitute the fabric of the country's politico-economic regime.[14]

To comprehend the context in which the Israeli politico-economic system evolved one has to deliberate upon the conditions of the country, the times in which it came into being, and the people who shaped it.

In other words, it can be argued that the intensive intervention of the state in the economy has its roots in the peculiar conditions in which Israel was established. The Israeli state qualifies for the description of a giant by virtue of its domination of thc national cconomy. The state has been rather strong and ubiquitous in nature from its inception. Like other new states, the lack of resources in the private sector dictated centralized public institutions to marshal resources and build infrastructure. Israel had the additional motivations of a Zionist theory (a strong state to protect the people who had suffered from two millennia of statelessness, plus a significant amount of socialism to protect the weak) and the Central and Eastern-European models of strong states to inspire its national founders. On-going hostilities and mass immigration added to the powers of the state, as did the Diaspora, which was willing to loan and donate money directly to state and the national institutions closely associated with it. The Zionist attempt to settle the Jews in Palestine encountered a market-failure; that is, a competitive private sector was unable to accomplish the colonization of large numbers of immigrant Jews. This failure gave birth to a particular brand of interventionist statism that was strengthened by converging requirements/needs and ideologies. In other words, the practical needs of nation building seem to have been well served by the leading (socialist) 'Pragmatic Zionist' ideological stances of the period. The state's manipulation of the economy served both party and political purposes. This explains the survival of the domineering statist system for as long as it did.

Yet, the instruments that the state employed ironically exposed it to increasing demands from the public as the discretionary interventionist powers of the government invited political pressures from the members of the public, who tried to exploit them to attain their own private economic ends.[15] The gradual demise of statism is due partly to the self-liquidating nature of some of the state's instruments for intervention, and partly to successful economic development. Moreover, both the Left and the Right now support the decrease in state power. Today, the Israeli economy is much less interventionist. Nevertheless, despite the long-run trend to liberalisation, the government's direct involvement remains considerable. The argument put forth is that in the absence of a major security or economic calamity, the trend away from interventionism will probably continue at an accelerated/ enhanced rate. The vacillations/fluctuations discernible in politics and in social organizations rarely, relapse to previously occupied positions. Circumstances change, societies evolve, and the solutions of the past are very often no longer applicable to today's problems. Statism may have outlived its role in Israel and therefore, has been abandoned. However, as far away from it as the Israeli society may move, it may have to face the question of how to respond to the requirements and sentiments for which statism was initially the solution and which has long remained its justification.

The Cultural Divergence

The widely accepted view that the primary conflict within Israeli-Jewish culture and society is between religious and secular Jews and their culture could be misleading. Instead, the contention is that there are three, rather than two, cultures and publics: the religio-political culture, the consumerist-post-modernist culture, and the secular-Jewish culture.[16] Under the rubric of religio-political culture are two basic sub-cultures: that of the religious-Zionists and that of the Haredim (the ultra-orthodox). At its heart, it is driven by a series of beliefs, which could be summarized as follows: Judaism is to be understood primarily as a halakhic system[17] comprised of beliefs and norms that pervade all aspects of public as well as private life. Rabbis who are educated in sacred text are the arbiters of this system and they are, therefore, the final arbiters of all matters of any importance in public or private life. The second culture prevalent in Israeli Jewish society is the consumerist post-modernist culture, which is basically indifferent, and at some levels hostile, to the Jewish tradition. At the private level, its extreme adherents are those who abjure any observance of traditional Jewish ritual and custom. It is politically represented by post-Zionism, that is, opposition to the notion of Israel as a Jewish state and replacing it with a state for all its citizens. Secular-Jewish culture is found among a variety of people. Most members of this group are affected by either post-modernist or politico-religious culture, or some of them, by both. This has led its opponents to deny its existence or its capacity to survive. However a secular Jew has been described as one who at least in some aspects of his life and most likely in the area of public policy choices, makes decisions independently of halakha or of rabbinic decisions. The Jewish secularist is likely to comprehend Jewish history as a series of events that can be understood without reference to God's intervention. While the other two sub-cultures flourish, the secular Jewish subculture is alive, but ailing. The secular-Jewish public lacks an articulated high culture. There have been some efforts to formulate a contemporary ideology for secular Jewishness; the works of Eliezer Schweid is noteworthy in this respect. [18] Gavison clearly explicates this category of secular Jews as:

> It is the opponents of halakha, (who are also) committed to the idea of Israel as a Jewish nation-state, who must explain the particular content of Jewish nationalism. They are the ones who must transmit this answer to the new generation of Israelis who didn't arrive here by virtue of the Zionist revolution as a consequence of a deep existential struggle with their personal identity. If they don't have an answer, we can anticipate two possible developments: the vacuum will be filled with Jewish religious content, with all its separatist principles, or all Israeli-Jews will be a people who speak Hebrew (and among some of them their Hebrew is poor and defective), but lacking any special orientation to the national Jewish culture.[19]

In response to critics, who cast doubts about the existence of a category of secular-Jews,[20] the likes of Gavison, Schweid and others argue that strengthening secular-Jewishness is essential to securing a Jewish state and in order to compete with the other two sub-cultures, secular Jewishness must be explicitly articulated and expressed; the first step toward this situation being the self-recognition by secular Jews that they constitute a third force in Israel's 'Kulturkampf.'

The Democracy Debates

The debates on democracy centre on the premise that Israel is a divided society where the primary fault line exists between the Jews and the Arabs of Israel. In the context of this rupture, academic debates have brought to the fore the categories of ethnic democracy and 'ethnocracy' to illustrate the Israeli case. Sammy Smooha's ethnic democracy model seeks to explain the place and outlook of Israeli Palestinians; expose the issues, tensions, and contradictions in such democracies and the strategies employed for dealing with them.[21] Ethnic democracy is a system in which two contradictory principles operate: the democratic principle, providing for equal rights and equal treatment of all citizens, and the ethnic principle, making for fashioning a homogenous nation-state and privileging the ethnic majority. As such, in such regimes, the majority's dominance is institutionalised alongside democratic procedures. Smooha's discussion naturally focuses on the particulars of the relationship between the Jewish majority and the Israeli Palestinian minority. The latter, Smooha argues, are dissatisfied with their minority status. Although they accept the territorial and political integrity of Israel within the pre-1967 borders, they find the existing terms of coexistence with the Jews unreasonable. He locates increasing friction between Jews and Israeli Palestinians in large measure because of growing democratisation. The Palestinians in Israel are one of the marginal groups who find it feasible to demand their rights and equality. The Jewish reaction is not sympathetic because for them the Palestinian demands seem to be too radical. Smooha suggests that it is possible to neutralize the conflict by reforming Israel's ethnic democracy with a New Zionism that accepts the rights of the Palestinian in historical Palestine as equal to those of the Jews. He is of the opinion that this is a reasonable solution that can preserve Israel as both democratic and Jewish-Zionist. Smooha argues that the Israeli case demonstrates the viability of an ethnic democracy as a distinct type of democracy in deeply divided societies.

In response to Smooha's model, a group of scholars, Nadim Rouhana, As'ad Ghanem and Oren Yiftachel contest the categorization of Israel as an ethnic democracy and prefer to use the term, ethnocracy, instead. [22]

Their critique addresses several key problems in the ethnic democracy model that revolve around the impossibility of establishing an ethnic democracy in a bi-ethnic context. Rouhana and others, challenge the assertion that a structural, state sanctioned, and long-term inequality of ethnic rights can coexist with democratic rule. They also contend that Israel cannot be analysed as an archetype case of majority-minority relations, as implied in Smooha's work, given the continuing Judaisation of the country. In other words, the analysis of Arab-Jewish relations in Israel cannot be neatly isolated from the historical process during which Palestinian-Arabs lost control over their land and became a minority, or from the on-going immigration, citizenship and land laws and policies which continue to deepen Jewish domination. The thrust of their criticism of ethnic democracy model is the presence of civil inequality and lack of minority consent, ethnic exclusion, and problems in the definition of state boundaries. The contention is that ethnic democracy is both a theoretical and empirical impossibility. Though Israel possesses several hallmarks of a democratic system but given the overriding ethnocentric nature of the system and the mixture of democratic and non-democratic components, they suggest an analytical distinction between state democratic features and structures. While they acknowledge that the situation has not been static and that improvements have occurred in the situation of Israel's Arab citizens, however, these improvements—important as they are—have not undermined the cornerstones of Israel's ethnocratic regime and have thus failed to effectively advance Arab-Jewish equality. As such, this group of scholars suggest that concepts such as ethnocracy or ethnic state capture the essence of the Israeli political structure more effectively and appropriately, by portraying the regime as neither democratic nor authoritarian.

In Lieu of Conclusions

It is widely perceived that there has been a perceptible shift in the Israeli-Palestinian conflict in the first decade of the twenty-first century with deep consequences for the Israeli society and polity. The Middle East peace process has not made any significant progress since the

Camp David Accords and with subsequent developments such as the outbreak of the second Intifada, expansion of settlements in the West Bank and the Gaza Strip, stalemate in the peace process and the protracted nature of the conflict, questions are now being raised as to whether this is in fact an ethnic conflict rather than a territorial one. Moreover, the heightened sense of insecurity has permeated the Israeli-Arabs, who feel that unlike the 1990s, when Israeli society was more open than ever to liberal values, a decade later Israeli Jews are less comfortable with including its Palestinian citizens as part of their Israeli polity. In the regional context, the Arab uprisings may have significant repercussions' for the state of Israel as Arab states and societies are experiencing a transitional and in some cases a turbulent phase in their history. While the common view is that the uprisings in the Arab countries have not centred around the Palestinian issue, yet, it is also equally widely felt that the situation as it unfolds will have an impact on the peace process as the new governments that emerge will have to at least appear more sensitive to popular opinion in their countries. The Arab Spring may herald a new era where peace will have to more explicitly seen to be made between peoples of the region if it is to be credible, adding another aspect of difficulty to an already troubled peace process. Thus, one of the paradoxes of the events of 2011 is that they could make peace between Israel and the Palestinians both more essential and challenging.

Israel appears more similar to Western countries than it really is. It is in actuality embedded in Judaism, Jewish history and Zionism. To compound difficulties in construing the Jewish state is the fact that constant interaction with Arab actors over a century, including not only conflict but also interpenetration and cooperation, strongly influences important parts of the Israeli society. Israel is in a state of transition. The essay indicates a sense of movement and points to serious complications/ruptures and perhaps momentous transformations in the economy, politics, citizenship, religious/secular divisions, and Jewish/Arab relationships. It is specifically this sense of dynamic change that needs to be emphasised. The state of Israel as it stands today is distinctly different from the one that was formed in 1948. The essay depicts a state in flux and concludes with the view that the innate struggle between the traditional forces in the Israeli social and political systems and the new/evolving tendencies toward liberalisation may unavoidably further weaken the power of the state.

Notes

1. The Kibbutz refers to a collective community in Israel that was traditionally based on agriculture. They began as utopian communities based on collectivism and Zionism, however, in recent times some of them have been privatised and changes have been incorporated in the communal lifestyle. The Moshav refers to a type of Israeli settlement, a type of cooperative agricultural community of individual farms pioneered by the Labour Zionists during the second aliyah (wave of Jewish immigration) in the early 20th century. The Hisdradut is the organisation of Trade Unions in Israel, established in 1920; it became one of the most powerful institutions of the Israeli state.
2. For a detailed discussion see S.Smooha, "Is Israel Western?" In Eliezer Ben Rafael and Yitzhak Sternberg,(eds.), *Comparing Modernities: Pluralism versus Homogeneity: Essays in Homage to Shmuel N. Eisenstadt*, (Leiden and Boston: Brill Academic Publishers, 2005), pp. 413-442; Yaron Ezrahi, "Democratic Politics and Culture in Modern Israel: Recent Trends", In Ehud Sprinzak and Larry Diamond (eds.), *Israeli Democracy under Stress,* (Boulder, Co.: Lynne Rienner, 1993), pp. 255-272.
3. See Joel S. Migdal, "Society Formation and the Case of Israel", in in Michael Barnett,(Ed), *Israel in Comparative Perspective: Challenging the Conventional Wisdom, (*Albany, N.Y.: State University of New York Press, 1997), pp. 173-197.
4. G. Sheffer, "Has Israel Really Been a Garrison Democracy? Sources of Change in Israeli Democracy," *Israel Affairs*, vol. 3, no.1, 1996; Yaron Ezrahi, "Democratic Politics and Culture in Modern Israel: Recent Trends," in Ehud Sprinzak and Larry Diamond, (Eds.), *Israeli Democracy Under Stress*, Boulder, Colorado: Lynne Reiner, 1993.
5. For a comprehensive discussion on issues related to citizenship in contemporary Israel see Gershon Shafir and Yoav Peled, *Being Israeli: The Dynamics of Multiple Citizenship*, (Cambridge: Cambridge University Press, 2002); G. Sheffer, " Individualism vs. National Coherence: The Current Discourse on Sovereignty, Citizenship and Loyalty," in *Israel Studies*, vol 2, no 2, Fall 1997, pp.118-145.
6. The Sephardi Jews refers to the descendants of the Jews who lived in the Iberian

Peninsula before their expulsion in the late 15th century. The other main group of Jews are the Ashkenazim ——the Jews who lived in the Rhineland valley and in neighbouring France before their migration eastward to Slavic lands (e.g., Poland, Lithuania, Russia) after the Crusades (11th–13th century) and their descendants.

7. The Israeli Arabs are non-Jewish Israeli citizens whose cultural and linguistic heritage or ethnic identiy is Arab and their vernacular is the Palestinian dialect of Arabic.
8. See Gershon Shafir and Yoav Peled, *Being Israeli: The Dynamics of Multiple Citizenship*, (Cambridge: Cambridge University Press, 2002).
9. Post Zionism is a term applied to a current set of critical positions that problematize Zionist discourse and the historical narratives and social representations that it produced. Like the term Zionism, post Zionism encompasses a variety of positions. To its critics, post Zionism presents a challenge to the basic principles and values of Zionism but to its advocates it is a necessary prerequisite to Israel's emergence as a fully democratic state.
10. Haredi is a term used to describe the most conservative form of Orthodox Judaism also referred to as the ultra-orthodox by outsiders.
11. Gershon Shafir and Yoav Peled, *Being Israeli: The Dynamics of Multiple Citizenship*, Cambridge: Cambridge University Press, 2002.
12. Charles S. Liebman, "Religion and Democracy in Israel", in *Israeli Democracy under Stress,* Ehud Sprinzak and Larry Diamond, (Eds.),(Boulder, Co.: Lynne Rienner, 1993), pp.273-292.
13. See Yonathan Shapiro, "The Historical Origins of Israeli Democracy", in *Israeli Democracy under Stress,* (Eds.), Ehud Sprinzak and Larry Diamond, (Boulder, Co.: Lynne Rienner, 1993, pp. 65-81); Baruch Kimmerling, *The Invention and Decline of Israeliness: State, Society, and the Military, (*Berkeley: University of California Press, 2001), pp. 56-88; E. Kleiman, "The Waning of the Israeli *Etatisme*," *Israel Studies*, vol.2, no.2, 1997, pp.146-171. For further reading see Dan Horowitz and Moshe Lissak; *Trouble in Utopia: the Overburdened Polity of Israel,* (Albany, N.Y.: State University of New York Press, 1995) Chapters 2 and 3
14. For a background to the changes, see Michael Shalev, Labour *and the Political Economy of Israel*, (New York: Oxford University Press, 1992).
15. Michael Shalev, *Labour and the Political Economy of Israel*, (New York: Oxford University Press, 1992.)
16. For a detailed background of the evolution of Israel's political culture see Shlomo Avineri, *The Making of Modern Zionism: The Intellectual Origins of the Jewish State, (*New York: Basic Books). For a contemporary reading of the same see Boaz Evron *Jewish State or Israeli Nation?,* (Bloomington: Indiana University Press, 1995); C. S. Liebman, "Reconceptualizing the Culture Conflict among Israeli Jews," *Israel Studies*, vol.2, no.2, Fall 1997, pp. 172-189; Charles S. Liebman, "Religion

and Democracy in Israel", in *Israeli Democracy under Stress,* Ehud Sprinzak and Larry Diamond,(Eds) (Boulder, Co.: Lynne Rienner, 1993), pp.273-292; Asher Cohen, and Bernard Susser, *Israel and the Politics of Jewish Identity, (*Baltimore: Johns Hopkins University Press, 2000), pp. 1-72.

17. Halakha is the collective body of Jewish religious law, including Biblical law and later Talmudic and Rabbinic law.
18. See Naftali Rothenberg and Eliezer Schweid, (ed), *Jewish Identity in Modern Israel: Proceedings on Secular Judaism and Demcocracy,* (Jerusalem: Van Leer Institute, 2002).
19. Ruth Gavison," A Jewish and Democratic State Political Identity, Ideology and Law," in Rosen-Zvi, (ed) *Jewish and Democratic*, Tel Aviv University Press, 1996, p.216; also see Ruth Gavison, "Jewish and Democratic? A Rejoinder to the "Ethnic Democracy" Debate", *Israel Studies* vol.4,no 1, 1999,pp. 44-72.
20. This category includes the likes of Baruch Kimmerling and Boaz Evron. See B. Kimmerling, *The Invention and Decline of Israeliness: State, Society and Military*, (Berkeley and Los Angeles: University of California Press, 2001); Boaz Evron, *Jewish State or Israeli Nation?, (*Bloomington: Indiana University Press, 1995).
21. S. Smooha, "Ethnic Democracy: Israel as an Archetype," *Israel Studies*, vol.2, no.2, 1997, pp.198-241; S. Smooha, 'Class, Ethnic, and National Cleavages and Democracy in Israel', in Ehud Sprinzak and Larry Diamond, (Eds.), *Israeli Democracy under Stress,* Boulder, Co.: Lynne Rienner, 1993, pp. 309-342.
22. As'ad Ghanem, Nadim Rouhana and Oren Yiftachel, "Questioning "Ethnic Democracy: A Response to Sammy Smooha," *Israel Studies*, vol 3, no.2, 1998, pp.253-267; For further reading see Nadim Rouhana and As'ad Ghanem,"The Crisis of Minorities in Ethnic States: The Case of Palestinian Citizens in Israel", *International Journal of Middle East Studies* 30 1998, pp. 321-346; Raphael Cohen-Almagor, ed., *Israeli Democracy at the Crossroads,* (London: Routledge, 2005), pp. 117-136; Alan Dowty "Is Israel Democratic? Substance and Semantics in the Ethnic Democracy Debate", *Israel Studies* vol. 4 no. 2, 1999: pp.1-15.; Oren Yiftachel, *Ethnocracy: Land and Identity Politics in Israel/Palestine,* (Philadelphia: University of Pennsylvania Press, 2006).

10. The Elusive Turmoil in Iran: *The Prospect of Change in the Islamic Republic*

Kingshuk Chatterjee

Introduction

The Islamic Republic of Iran was not engulfed in the turmoil that the so-called Arab Spring turned out to be, but only just. Many of the factors that are now believed to have caused the social and political upheavals across the Middle East – high rates of inflation and unemployment, high levels of public discontent – were present in Iran as well. So much so, that at one stage Tehran was somewhat hesitant to voice its support for the ouster of Mubarak, lest it encouraged disaffected Iranian youth to take to the *Maidan-e Azadi* in Tehran. A lot of these rumblings had surfaced and subsided around the elections of 2009, when the principal challenger to the incumbent President Mahmoud Ahmedinejad, Mir-Hossein Mousavi, led the public demonstrations alleging electoral fraud, which prompted a severe crackdown by the ruling elite that was unequalled in its severity for over a decade. It is not altogether a far-fetched proposition that the very forces which occasioned the "disturbances" in 2009 happened to resurface in 2013, carrying Hassan Rouhani to power. Hence, unlike in the case of some of her neighbours, no social upheaval came and swept away the Islamic Republic, but neither did the regime weather the winds of change unscathed – the regime remained, but the government was toppled in 2013.

This paper looks into the nature of the body-politic and dispensation of power in the Islamic Republic in the light of the 2009 elections, in order to assess the nature, scope and extent of tensions between the regime and the people. It begins with the turmoil of 2009, and then goes on to a brief sketch of the Iranian body-politic, followed by a look at the roles of the principal stake-holders in the turbulent period around the elections of 2009. It then proceeds to contextualise the turmoil within the larger matrix of economic downturn from 2008, and analyse the impact on political alignments in the Islamic Republic. The paper also assesses the character of the shifts in political discourse in tandem with the changing alignments, and then goes on to argue that Iran successfully eluded the turmoil precisely because the Islamic Republic accommodates the principle of popular sovereignty to a much greater extent than almost any of its neighbours.

The 2009 Elections: The Turmoil that did not become Turbulence

In June 2009, Iranians went to the polls to elect their President for a four-year term. Contrary to standard practice in the Islamic Republic, the Ministry of Interior declared the incumbent President Mahmoud Ahmedinejad as the victor shortly after the polls closed, with over 62% of the votes. For the next few weeks, first time since the Islamic Revolution of 1979, Iranians took to the streets to dispute the electoral outcome, with the principal challenger to the incumbent President, the former Prime Minister Mir-Hossein Mousavi, lodging a formal request for investigation into irregularities and then leading massive demonstrations in the capital city of Tehran, alleging that the elections had been "stolen". The discontent continued even after the Rahbar (Supreme Leader) 'Ali Khamenei endorsed Ahmedinejad's victory and warned the protesters against dire consequences.[1] Brutal crackdown followed on protesters, with massive numbers of uniformed regulars and riot police being accompanied by non-uniformed vigilantes of the *basij* militia on motor-cycles who rained down not merely on public demonstrations,[2] but also allegedly on supporters of Mousavi in their homes.[3] Little news of the protests filtered through mainstream media such as the newspapers like *Ettela'at, Keyhan, Hamshahri, Jomhuri Islami*, and the official news agency IRNA, and even the internet services were disrupted presumably with a clear intent to regulate the flow of information about the protests. Cyber-savvy Iranians reached out for proxy internet servers in order both to stay informed about what was happening, as also let out the enormity and the brutality of the crackdown.[4] Both the two contenders who came closest to the incumbent, Hossein Mousavi and Mehdi Karroubi, were eventually put under house arrest where they remained all through the second term of Ahmedinejad era, and continue to languish till this essay went to the press.

A substantial number of Iranians and western observers have expressed their doubt about the verdict, both in the conventional media and on the internet.[5] Quite apart from the debate in the media and cyber world, a number of more serious and informed contributions have pondered over the veracity of the verdict.[6] The principal reason for the debate happens to be the hurry with which the verdict was announced – Ahmedinejad was declared the winner within hours of the election coming to a close, with about 85% of the votes being cast. It almost seemed to the critics of the regime that the Iranian establishment could barely wait to announce a verdict that it desired, lest a different verdict emerged from the polls themselves. Reformist candidates Hossein Mousavi, Mehdi Karroubi as well as candidates close to the present dispensation, like Mohsen Rezai went on to accuse Ahmedinejad's camp (i.e. the government) of fraudulent practices, including polling in several regions (viz. provinces of Mazandaran and Yazd) at over 100% in terms of the total population. Ali Akbar Mohtashipur, a former Minister of the Interior, claimed in a television interview that he possesses documents showing that in at least seventy constituencies more than 140% of eligible voters were recorded as having voted; and that the number of votes for Ahmadinejad recorded in these constituencies was 110% of total eligible voters.[7] Strong insinuations emerged from the Mousavi camp that the polls were rigged. Hence, public demonstrations carried out on the streets of (primarily) Tehran coined the concept that came to dominate most of the discussion since then – *Entekhab-e Gumshudeh* (the Missing Election).

The official explanations provided by the *Showra-ye Negahban* (Council of Guardians – the body that undertakes the screening of candidates for elections in the Islamic Republic, and adjudicates on all disputes pertaining to elections) contended that much of the higher-than-possible percentage was owing to the fact that Iranian Presidential electoral constituencies are not run on the strict principle of regional domicile. An Iranian citizen may cast his vote from any part of the country that he may happen to be in at the time of the polls.[8] This does not explain why there would be such a huge surplus of votes in Mazandaran and Yazd (the heartland of the reformist movement under Khatami), without a corresponding deficit showing up in other provinces elsewhere. A far better explanation to what happened in 2009, consistent with the patterns of previous Iranian Presidential elections as also the last few *Majlis* elections, would be that the outcome was possibly not rigged,[9] but the margin in all possibility was (which would explain not merely the announcement of the verdict, but also of the margin within a few hours of the polls closing).

The labels remained stuck, though, both in the international media ("stolen") and in the popular imagination ("*gumshudeh*") – presumably because of the visual impact of demonstrations by thousands of Iranians, predominantly the youth, and the heavy-handed crackdown by the regular police as well as the vigilantes – thereby undermining the legitimacy of Ahmedinejad in popular perception during his second term in office. Commentary in the international media emphasised that Ahmedinejad was, in fact, a close acolyte of ‘Ali Khamenei, the Supreme Leader – and thus it was virtually self-explanatory why the establishment stood behind Ahmedinejad, and helped in the ‘disappearance’ of the popular mandate.[10] The fact that Hossein Mousavi had a past with Khamenei,[11] made suggestions of Mousavi's unacceptability vis-à-vis Khamenei an equally useful (and perhaps not altogether incorrect) talking point. A more informed opinion argued that Khamenei's endorsement of Ahmedinejad was in fact going to reduce the President to rubber-stamp, since his legitimacy now depended on the *Rahbar*. Ahmedinejad's selection of his cabinet with people he was not particularly close to, and who were known acolytes of Khamenei, reinforced this impression.[12]

The debate on the validity of the election verdict clouded some important aspects of the political language in use around the election of 2009. Was the assertion of dissent by the losing candidates an act of dissent (which, under the constitution of the Islamic Republic, is legitimate) or dissidence (which is illegitimate)? Did the demonstrations warrant the kind of violent crackdown that followed, and if they did not then why did the crackdown happen? If the demonstrations were merely dissent and not dissidence, clearly the crackdown was uncalled for – and it might be argued this was merely an attempt by a very authoritarian government to silence the voice of the people. If on the other hand, the acts constituted dissidence with the establishment, then the crackdown could be shrouded with the legitimacy that is accorded to an act of self-preservation.

It is somewhat interesting to observe that to start with the ruling establishment of the Islamic Republic did not quite consider the initial demonstrations as either illegitimate or unacceptable. Despite having endorsed the re-election of Ahmedinejad on 12th June, Khamenei suggested to the Guardians Council on the 15th of June to consider a recount within 10 days,[13] to which the Guardians acceded the day after.[14] Although these were generally held in the western media to be acts of posturing (which may or may not have been correct) calculated to buy time,[15] these were momentous decisions and were correctly understood as such on the streets of Tehran – for never before had the Guardian's Council bowed down to what was effectively public pressure, however briefly. The Mousavi camp was quick to realise that there was an opening, and immediately demanded that the Guardians overturn the initial verdict.[16] The Guardians however were adamant in not doing so, conceding only a recount of specific cases of fraudulent practice.[17]

It was only after a full week of relentless demonstrations that the regime finally closed its ranks behind the verdict, when in course of his Friday sermon, Khamenei endorsed the verdict a second time, and warned opposition demonstrators with consequences if they persisted with their protests.[18] He was cautious enough, however, to not question the right of the people to entertain suspicions about electoral manipulations, conceding that the regime was becoming corrupted in some of its ways. He insinuated however, that the demonstrations were the product of a malicious conspiracy by foreign powers (specifically Britain) to undermine the Iranian people's faith in their political system.[19] He warned off the protesters and the opposition leaders that a challenge to the legitimacy of the regime on the streets was not acceptable, because that would undermine democracy in the country. From that point on, the crackdown got even more severe even as demonstrations continued relentlessly. Although, in absence of official figures, it is not possible to give any firm idea of the number of those arrested, several hundreds are known to have been killed (including the nephew of Hossein Mousavi) owing to heavy-handed repression, and several thousands were behind bars within 6 months of the disputed verdict. The protests continued well after the formal inauguration of Ahmedinejad's second term on 5th August 2009, and intermittent demonstrations were carried out as late as 2010. Restrictions were imposed on the movements of Mousavi and Karroubi, and eventually both were arrested on 14th February 2011, when the two former presidential candidates urged the Iranians to demonstrate in solidarity with the Arab protesters across the region.[20] They continue to be under house arrest even today.

Dispensation of Power in the Islamic Republic: Footfalls of Authoritarianism?

Why did the demonstrations continue even after the election of Ahmedinejad was realised by everyone as a *fait accompli*? Why did Mousavi and Karroubi, both of whom were actually associated with the Islamic Revolution and high offices in the Islamic Republic at different times willing to cast their lot with the protesters?[21] So far as the regime was concerned, the demonstrations appeared to pose an existential threat and had to be ruthlessly subjugated. The threat posed, however, was much less to Ahmedinejad himself than the institutional complex that constitutes the political establishment of Tehran. Thus, while the regime was willing to admit the possibility that there might have been some electoral malpractices, and even conceded a partial recount, in demanding annulment of the verdict the Mousavi camp was basically assailing not only the highly suspect role played by the Ministry of Interior, but also the Guardians Council which endorsed the legitimacy of the verdict. Even if the verdict was sham, (which in all probability it was not), as custodians of thc Islamic character of the state, the Guardians would not have been able to admit to complicity in such malpractice without undermining the regime itself.

The institutional character of the Islamic Republic was heavily influenced by Iran's experience of the Pahlavi monarchy. During the Pahlavi era (1925-79), most *Majlis* (Parliament) elections were rigged almost as a matter of routine, ensuring a pliant majority that would rubber-stamp any measure solicited by the Shah who made use of the state apparatus to promote the interests of the ruling elite.[22] Hence a number of Iranians developed a deep-seated misgiving about the efficacy of the principle of separation of powers between elected legislative and executive organs of government. In 1979, therefore, after the Islamic Revolution overthrew the Pahlavis and the new regime was being shaped, a simple supremacy of the legislative organ was ruled out. While the principle of elective legislative and executive authorities was retained at the national level, Ayatollah Khomeini's theory of *Vilayat-e Faqih* (Rule of the Jurist) was foisted on this institutional combine from above. The consequent amalgam of democratic and so-called 'theocratic' features has rendered the exact location of popular sovereignty slightly ambiguous.[23]

Chief among the democratic elements in the Islamic Republic of Iran is the popularly elected *Rais* (President). Elected for a four-year term allowing only one consecutive re-election, the President appoints a council of ministers to help him discharge the functions of his office, which include determining programmes and policies of the government and implementation of laws passed by the *Majlis*.[24] Apart from the office of the President, the *Majlis-e Showra-ye Islami* (Islamic Consultative Assembly), the supreme legislative organ in the Islamic Republic, is also directly elected by the people under a system of universal adult franchise. It is authorised to make laws pertaining to all matters within the compass of the state, provided the laws do not run contrary to the essence (*usul al-*

din) and injunctions (*ahkam*) of the official religion i.e. Twelver Shi'ism, and are in conformity to the spirit of the constitution. In a bid to establish a democratic check on the executive, the Presidential council of ministers have to be individually approved by the *Majlis* before they assume their responsibilities. Further, at any stage, a motion of no-confidence can be brought against ministers individually or collectively, which may even lead to their removal.

However, given the experience of abuse of executive authority and subversion of the *Majlis* under the Pahlavis, the Constitution of the Islamic Republic has created an institutional complex where powers of the elected executive and legislative institutions are circumscribed by the powers and functions of a set of non-representative institutions and bodies. Chief among these is the office of the *Rahbar* (Supreme Leader or Guide), the highest constitutional authority in the land despite not being democratically elected by the people.[25] Further, there are the *Showra-ye Negahban* (Guardians Council) and the *Majme'-ye Tashkhish-e Maslihat-e Nizam* (Council for Determination of Expediency of the System, i.e. Expediency Council). [26] The Guardians Council is a non-representative body of twelve-members that circumscribes the authority of the *Majlis* – six being *fuqaha* (jurists) nominated by the Rahbar and six specialists in different branches of secular law appointed by the *Majlis*.[27] The Council for Determination of Expediency of the System, i.e. Expediency Council, was set up to prevent deadlock between the representative *Majlis* and the unrepresentative Guardians. Comprising of thirty odd members (some ex officio but mostly nominated by the *Rahbar*), the Expediency Council is authorised to resolve conflicts or disputes over legislation between the *Majlis* and the Guardians, and provide a binding resolution.

While all the representative and non-representative bodies are directly subject to the authority of the *Rahbar*, the office of the *Rahbar* itself is supervised by the *Majlis-e Khobregan* (Assembly of Experts, hereafter Experts), a body of eighty-odd members directly elected by the people for a term of eight years. Meeting at least once in every six months, the Experts are responsible for the selection, supervision and removal of the Leader – thereby allowing for the institutional mechanism to keep the *Rahbar* himself in check.

The institutional complex brought into being by the Islamic revolution in the body-politic of Iran was, clearly, devised with the express purpose of preventing any single institution from becoming powerful enough to dominate the rest. Even the office of the *Rahbar*, the repository of the greatest range of powers in the Islamic Republic, was used sparingly during the Khomeini years (1979-89) primarily to maintain a balance between the various political forces and government organs, rather than to be politically proactive.

In absence of any single centre of authority, the Islamic Republic of Iran has evolved into a polycratic system characterised by an unrelenting struggle for power among the *Rahbar*, the President, the *Majlis* and the Guardians where each has proven perfectly willing to align with everyone else for the short term. Hence the Rafsanjani Presidency (1989-97) was marked by close cooperation between the *Rahbar* and President but bitter opposition from the *Majlis*; the Khatami years (1997-2005) by contrast had the *Rahbar* align himself with the Guardians against the President and the *Majlis*; the Ahmedinejad era (2005-2013) was characterised by the President being locked into combat with all the other three organs. A very telling quip about Iran's body-politic runs, Iran is probably the only country in the world where a directly elected President is actually the leader of the opposition.

But then, what of sovereignty? Where does it rest? Despite the fact that the fifth chapter of the Iranian Constitution deals with "the Sovereignty of the People and the Powers Thereby Conferred," *prima facie,* it is tempting to argue that the subordination of the directly elected President and the Parliament to the unrepresentative institutions of the *Rahbar* and the Guardians makes a compelling case that sovereignty does not lie in the people. If a further question is posed as to where does it lie, an apparently simple answer is often given – only Allah wields absolute sovereignty (*hakimiat-e mutlaq*); i.e. the sovereignty of the people is subject to the parameters set by God.[28] It would be wrong, however, to be tempted by the simplistic conclusion. In truth, the actual and exact relationship between the limits set by God (*huddud al-lah*) and the legislative competence of the people is not definitively settled – the constitution clearly lays down that the sovereignty of the people cannot be subordinated to the particular interests of any individual or group of people.[29] There is no clear indication as to what constitutes the 'limits set by God' except the rather vague idea of Islamic law – vague, because there is no single definitive and immutable standard even of that, in Iran or elsewhere. Indeed, in the Islamic Republic, it is left to the *'ulema* hierocracy (of which the *Rahbar* is taken to be the highest functionary) versed in Islamic law to decide on such matters,[30] provisions about the actual act of legislation endorses the principle that regulations binding the people have to emanate from the people themselves. While an unrepresentative body (the Guardians Council) can pronounce on whether a law conforms to the essence of the Islam, they are not authorised to make any laws – not unlike unrepresentative bodies (viz. judiciary, constitutional courts, etc) in other countries pronouncing on the constitutionality of any act of legislation, but unable to initiate any legislation themselves.

There remains, nevertheless, an element of ambivalence in the way popular sovereignty is understood by the members of the body-politic in Iran, principally as a consequence of the polycratic character of the Islamic Republic. With no single organ of the state powerful enough to overshadow all the others, post-revolutionary Iranian politics has been characterised by social groups and political factions (sometimes coinciding, sometimes not) jostling with each other either to gain leverage within the system, trying to dominate as many of the political organs as possible. In the course of this relentless endeavour to establish their dominance within the body-politic, all the various political forces have tried to engage with the problematic question about the exercise of sovereign power, if only to limit the power at the disposal of the various organs at different points of time.[31] As a consequence, there is yet to emerge a definitive formulation of not so much the idea of popular sovereignty, as its contours and parameters.

The principal protagonists of the debate on popular sovereignty in the Islamic Republic can be classified into two camps. Votaries of the minimalist position who argue that while the principle of popular sovereignty be accepted, its exercise should be left in the hands that could be trusted to carry forward the revolutionary principles that informed the founding of the Islamic Republic – i.e. the generation that brought about and shaped the revolutionary regime and those that have been among its principal beneficiaries. For the purpose of ease in understanding, this essay would refer to the champions of the minimalist position as the Conservatives.[32] On the other hand are those who favour a maximalist position on popular sovereignty, who believe the people must be allowed a greater voice in the Islamic Republic for it to strike deeper roots than it has done so far. They argue that the revolution in 1979 was a social revolution that was brought about by the people as a whole, who were then disenfranchised during the 1980s as protagonists of the minimalist position came to dominate the levers of power in the beleaguered days of the Iraq War. This position has come to gain considerable support from the generation that has come after the revolution, and has had little tangible benefits that could have endeared them to it. For the purpose of this essay, this platform would be referred to as the Reformists.[33]

In large measure these questions were opened up by the *Dovvom-e Khordad* movement (loosely spoken of as the Reformist movement), which aimed at virtually re-founding the Islamic Republic during the Khatami era, before the rearguard action of the minimalists stalled its momentum. The Ahmedinejad era that followed, interestingly, began with a successful fight-back by the protagonists of the minimalist position dominating most of the various organs of the state (viz. the office of the Rahbar, the Guardians Council, the *Majlis,* and the President's office) culminating in the 2009 presidential election. When the supporters of Hossein Mousavi took to the streets, therefore, the minimalists got their act together, in order to save not so much the Islamic Republic as its minimalist version.

It is thus useful to understand the scope of the reform agenda to fully comprehend the Reformist interrogation of the minimalist position on popular sovereignty. To that we turn in the next section.

The Reform Agenda and the Lost Revolution

It is possible to locate the agenda of reform in Iranian politics in two different impulses occasioned by the same factor – the Iraq War (1980-88). For the actual survival of the Islamic Republic, the more urgent of the two impulses behind the reform agenda was undoubtedly the dismantling of the highly regulated war economy that had been erected by the war-time Prime Minister Mir-Hossein Mousavi. However, for the long term health of the country, the other impulse to dismantle the highly regulated social and political spaces that characterised wartime Iran was also considered equally significant. While the presidential tenure of Rafsanjani came to be associated principally with the reforms of the first sort, his successor Muhammad Khatami virtually came to personify the reformist agenda by embracing the cause of total structural reform following both the impulses.

The economic devastation caused by the Iraq War was not confined simply to the loss of 2.13 million lives. Hardships imposed by the war had considerably reduced the standard of living – shortage of foreign currency and the persisting need for war mobilisation, reduced imports of items of mass consumption, which were essential for meeting domestic shortages, by nearly 50% between 1983 and 1988.[34] Additionally, despite having kept on raising indirect taxes and the price of state-run public utilities in order to meet its budget deficit, in 1989 Iran had a foreign debt of $12 billion on account of its short-term borrowing.[35] It was clear to a large segment of the Iranian establishment that a major structural overhaul of the country's economy was necessary for capital to be mobilized for the country to recover from devastation. The pragmatic Speaker of the *Majlis* and a close associate of Khomeini, Akbar Hashmi Rafsanjani, was elected to the President's office with the mandate to carry this programme of liberalisation through.[36]

For nearly a decade, the government had controlled domestic prices and imposed a wage ceiling, and kept the foreign exchange rates artificially overvalued, subjected imports to government allocation, required a variety of permits for establishing new industrial enterprises, refused to allow foreign investments in Iran, and provided subsidies for nearly all basic foodstuffs. It was premised upon foreign exchange liberalisation, decontrol of prices, elimination of subsidies and privatisation of state-owned enterprises.[37] The emphasis was now laid in changing the role of the state from intervention and control to supervision, thereby allowing private capital and market to increase investment in infrastructure and industrial output. The mercantile element of the *bazaar*, (with which the Iranian clergy enjoys close personal and social ties and which thus constitutes the bedrock of the so-called Conservative camp), favoured this part of Rafsanjani's agenda of dismantling of the command economy – hence Rafsanjani enjoyed full support of the Conservative dominated *Majlis* in the primary task of liberalisation, viz. deregulation of the economy. However, the Conservative support for economic liberalisation ran out by early 1990s, when the sanction-ridden Iranian economy compelled the government to raise direct taxes and costs of public utilities.

There was a more tricky part to the economic liberalisation story that came forth in course of the 1990s, stalled Rafsanjani's programme and hit Khatami with a vengeance. This was the need for a change in the role that the various industrial and economic conglomerates, i.e. the *bonyad-ha* (Foundations), had come to play in the Iranian economy. [38] During the Iraq War, the Foundations had played a crucial role in order to gear the economy towards the wartime needs. They also addressed the crisis in production occasioned by the flight of managerial professionals after the revolution necessitated nationalisation of major sectors of the economy, including all private banks, insurance companies, all heavy industries (including mining and metal industries as well as plane, ship and automobile manufacturing plants).[39] Being pivotal to the war economy, the Foundations enjoyed preferential allocation of resources and subsidies from the state, but did not score particularly high in terms of efficiency. For the economic recovery of the country, it was imperative for the state to reduce the burden of carrying on the Foundations on its back. However, a large number of the Foundations were under the control of the paramilitary Islamic Revolutionary Guards Corps (*Sepah-e Pasdaran-e Inqilab-e Islami*, hereafter, *Sepah*), and their reservists, the

Basij militia – the two organs which proved instrumental in mobilising the upwardly mobile educated youth of the lower and lower-middle class to the cause of the revolution.[40] At the end of the war, these foot-soldiers of the Islamic Revolution were left in command over considerable share of nationalised economic resources, for which the Foundations began to claim autonomy from government control by the time liberalisation was launched. It was always going to be a difficult task to get them to dissolve their stake in the economy. By 1990s, as the pressure for divestment mounted on Foundations run by the *Sepah* and the *Basij*, they began to join the Conservatives in resisting the agenda of economic reform.

The second component behind the reform agenda, dismantling the restrictive social and political order, was pushed, (and virtually personified in public imagination) by *Hojjatulislam* Sayyid Muhammad Khatami, Rafsanjani's Minister for Culture and Islamic Guidance, and then his successor as the President. Having been associated with the Ministry for Culture and Islamic Guidance during the purges of intellectual dissidents and political opponents in the early days of the Republic, Khatami favoured the idea of an Islamic state based on pluralist ideas that he saw as the essence of Islam and by 1987, even before the end of the Iran-Iraq war, Khatami began to call for a more open cultural regime – beginning the long-winded process of something like a *glasnost* in Iran.[41] Rafsanjani's liberalisation agenda gave Khatami the opportunity to carry out his policy of emancipation of Iran's public space: cable and satellite television was permitted in Iran for the first time during Khatami's tenure, exposing Iranians to western cultural influences; censorship was relaxed on both print and electronic media; the number of newspapers and journals published increased from 102 in 1988 to 369 in 1992.[42] In 1990 he even established a 'press jury' to investigate issues involving the media. The opposition to Khatami's attempt at liberalisation of the cultural policies of the Islamic Republic came from the Conservatives in the *Majlis* and the Guardians as also the socially-conservative element of the *Sepah*, or more exactly the *Basijis*.[43]

During the period 1990-92, the Conservative right grew determined in its opposition to Rafsanjani administration, partly because of the liberal cultural policies of Khatami, and partly because of the manner in which Rafsanjani was using the elective office of the presidency to push industrial policies that the conservatives disagreed with. The Conservative response was to attempt at the consolidation of other constitutional institutions, such as the Experts and the *Majlis* using the one institution they dominated ever since 1979, the Guardians. In July 1990, the Conservative-majority of the Experts decided to change two of the laws for the election to that body, which allowed the Guardians a decisive influence in the selection of eligible candidates.[44] As the reformists had almost no representation in the Guardians, this effectively guaranteed that the left could be excluded from the Experts as well. In December 1991, the Guardians clarified the reference to its 'supervisory' role in the *Majlis* elections of article 99 of the constitution to such an effect that they could use any statement critical of the institution or even the person of the *Rahbar* (i.e. Khomeini or Khamenei) to disqualify a candidate from running for *Majlis*. More significantly, even if such evidence was not readily available, any insinuation of opposition to the 'Islamic' nature of the regime would suffice. From this point onwards, the Guardians began to pre-empt as far as possible votaries of the 'reformist' position from the list of candidates.

A frontal assault was mounted on the liberalisation agenda by the Conservative-dominated *Majlis* in 1992, after successfully preventing prominent advocates of liberalisation from standing for election. Khatami was made to resign, and severe restrictions were reintroduced in Iran's social and cultural space by his successor, 'Ali Larijani. In a bid to enforce these restrictions at a time when the reformist Ministry of Interior was reluctant to do so, as also to win over the upwardly-mobile lower middle class youth, in 1992 the *Basijis* were effectively assigned a legally sanctioned role as enforcers of public morality.[45] After Rafsanjani's re-election in 1993, Conservative opposition to the agenda of liberalisation became even more vehement, successfully blocking almost all economic reform, and rolling back the opening up undertaken by Khatami.

When Khatami ran for the presidency, he had made it very clear to his campaign team that he was entering the arena primarily to openly discuss and raise awareness about the various structural reforms that he believed were necessary for the Islamic Republic to survive. The agenda for reforms that he drew up were anticipated and largely attempted by Rafsanjani himself. However, he went beyond the limits imposed by Rafsanjani's pragmatism and spoke about a systemic reform that proposed to substantively alter the Islamic regime.

Khatami spoke of the need to strengthen the representative institutions of the presidency and the *Majlis*, and reduce the diffusion of sovereign authority by limiting the right to exercise it in the representative institutions alone. At the same time, instead of concentrating all powers in the hands of the President as Rafsanjani tried to, Khatami spoke of devolving power to the various levels of local government that dated back to the pre-revolutionary era. This was, clearly, in complete opposition to the closed political system that the conservatives had been developing since the death of Khomeini, based upon the notion of *jame'h-ye vilayi* (a society that needs guidance from above). By speaking of giving power back to the society, Khatami meant to assail the legitimacy sought by the conservative establishment for their domination of the institutional complex of the Islamic Republic in the name of Islam. Because of the very nature of his agenda, Khatami emerged as the personification of all the various demands for reform that were circulating in Iran – hence the 'reformist' tag attached to the political movement *Nehzat-e Dovvom-e Khordad* (Second of Khordad Movement, after the date in Persian calendar on which the Presidential election of 1997 took place) that brought Khatami to power, with 20.7 million out of 29.7 million votes cast – an electoral landslide.

Khatami began with his agenda of strengthening the representative institutions of the Islamic Republic right away. In his first press conference five days after his election, he noted, "Our main goal is to institutionalise the rule of law and implement the constitution."[46] He went a step ahead in his inaugural address to the *Majlis*, when, paying homage to 'Ali Khamenei, he implied that the role of the *Rahbar* should be limited to supervisory-guidance, because he was the 'symbol' of national sovereignty and unity, drawing his power and legitimacy from the society as a whole and the constitution – i.e. he should not take sides.[47] The agenda received widespread support from a plethora of publications, newspapers and journals alike which challenged the protagonists of the minimalist idea of sovereignty by advocating for a supervisory *Rahbar* and a strong civil society. This was made easier by Khatami's proclamation that 'guidance' in the ministry of culture should not degenerate into guiding thinkers what to think.[48] In his bid to strengthen the representative organs of the Islamic Republic, Khatami championed the cause of subjecting every functionary of the Islamic regime to rule of law (*hokumat-e qanun*), saying that no one was above the laws of the state.[49] This was as much a criticism of the extra-legal position claimed by the *Rahbar*, as of the various institutions of the Islamic Republic dominated by the conservatives that claimed their legitimacy not from the people but either from the revolution or the *Rahbar*.

In February 1999, Khatami delivered on his campaign promise to hold the first ever elections for local governments in Iran: 'at one stroke 200,000 democratically elected officials entered the political structure, despite conservative … efforts to hold back the candidacy of the *Do-e Khordad* candidates.'[50] The successful empowerment of the people put wind in the reformist sail, securing not only a majority of the newly-elected local governments but also a decisive majority in the sixth *Majlis* elections of 2000.[51]

The reformist victory more or less completed the elected-unelected divide in Iranian body-politic with the balance of power in all elective institutions being held by the reformists and all non-elective organisations being dominated by the conservatives. In 2001, Khatami himself secured a victory even more resounding than the first one. Unlike Rafsanjani, who won his second term with a reduced vote share, Khatami actually increased his tally of votes to 78.3% of the total.

For all practical purposes, though, this constituted the high point of the reform movement under Khatami, because ever since the sixth *Majlis* came into being the conservative establishment dug its heels in opposition to Khatami every step of the way. The determined character of conservative opposition had as much to do with the economic reforms that Khatami was advocating as with his proposed political reforms. His 'Economic Recovery Plan', which paid special attention to the issue of unemployment, let the genie out of the bottle by undertaking the task of 'breaking monopolies' and regulating the Foundations.[52] The challenge was resumed in course of the Third Five Year Plan, (1999-2004) -- essentially a continuation of the economic liberalisation programme of the Rafsanjani era (viz. macroeconomic regulation, encouragement of domestic and foreign investment, reduction of public sector in the economy), but renewing the emphasis on making the giant economic entities of the Foundations fully accountable and open to public scrutiny.[53] As international oil prices, (hence oil revenue, the mainstay of the Iranian government) continued to fall consistently during the Khatami years,[54] the reformists ceaselessly attacked the virtual drain of government subsidies into similar other Foundations as well (viz. *Astan-e Qods* foundation) and demanded accountability of such organisations to the elected functionaries of the people.[55] As almost all of these Foundations are connected personally or organisationally with either the *Rahbar*, and/ or the conservative establishment, particularly the *Sepah*, the reformist agenda understandably alarmed the conservatives as an attempt to undermine their material basis.

The reformist-dominated sixth *Majlis* attempted to introduce a broad range of legislation – ranging from women's rights to human rights, from press freedom to increasing the potency of *Majlis* as the supreme legislative body in Iran. The reformists tried to revise laws about representation of the people, regarding parliamentary immunity for *Majlis* deputies vis-à-vis *Shari'ah* courts, according equal property rights to men and women, etc – putting on display the maximalist vision of popular sovereignty. More than fifty of such major attempts at reforming the Islamic Republic were successfully blocked by the Guardians by 2004.[56]

The Economic Downturn of 2008: Reformism's Second Wind?

By the time Khatami left office, the Guardians ensured Conservative domination of the seventh Majlis. This was as much because of the economic dislocation and distress caused by the economic liberalisation (particularly privatisation and price deregulation) among the lower-middle and lower class as the Guardian's exclusion of more than half of the reformists in the *Majlis*. Significantly, however, the traditional conservative formation aligned to the *bazaar* was joined by a relatively new entrant, the Basij-dominated Islamic populist *A'etelaf-e Abadgaran-e Iran-e Islami* (Alliance of Builders of Islamic Iran, usually referred to as the *Abadgaran*) led by the allies of the Mayor of Tehran, Mahmoud Ahmedinejad. In 2005 Presidential election, the virtually unknown Ahmedinejad trounced the veteran Rafsanjani, riding on the back of the support both of the *Basij* (from whose ranks he came) and the beneficiaries of his populist largesse as the Mayor of Tehran. In the four years that followed, Ahmedinejad happened to preside over perhaps the largest bounty in terms of favourable global oil prices in the history of the Islamic Republic.[57] Since the need to cut corners that was felt by Khatami and Rafsanjani disappeared almost overnight, Ahmedinejad went on to undo many of the more unpopular economic reforms undertaken by his two predecessors, and indulged in a sustained exercise of populism on the one hand, and a redistributive agenda on the other from which the paramilitary *Basij* and the *Sepah* emerged as the principal beneficiaries. In the process, however, most of the economic restructuring done by Rafsanjani and Khatami were undone, leaving Iran particularly unsuited to face the global economic downturn which began in 2008. The turmoil of 2009 was demonstrably the direct result of the impact of the meltdown on Iranian economy, and despite not having been successful it indicated to have been the beginning of Reformism's second wind in the Islamic Republic.

Ahmedinejad began as a darling of the Conservatives because he rolled back the social and cultural liberalisation that Khatami continued to push for. Universities, which were reputed to be the breeding grounds of reformism, were clamped down on; reform inclined newspapers were shut down; reformist sympathisers were persecuted and dissidents were prosecuted on largely trumped up charges. The visibility and activity of the *Basijis* successfully curbed the milieu of social and freedom that was quite palpable during the Khatami era. This earned Ahmedinejad quite a lot of opprobrium among the urban privileged and educated middle class, the one constituency of the reformists that remained intact.

However, favourable global world prices and Ahmedinejad's populist economic policies which such favourable prices helped underwrite guaranteed that Ahmedinejad rode reasonably high till 2008. In his public pronouncements, Ahmedinejad has repeatedly argued that the country's oil wealth belongs to the people as a whole, and that none of his predecessors had done anything to give them their due share. The redistributive agenda that he espoused as the Mayor of Tehran made him very popular among the Iranian underclass and the lower-middle class. Upon gaining power, therefore, Ahmedinejad began ostensibly to adopt a policy of distributing largesse to the underclass by means of doles, soft loans and most importantly the so-called "justice shares".[58] In order to generate employment, public works were undertaken at the centre and encouraged at the level of the *ostan-ha* (provinces). The most popular device Ahmedinejad resorted to in this context was to make fresh endowments to the provinces, each which could stimulate the corresponding regional economy with hand-outs from the centre – this, in fact, was one of the reasons why despite losing a large share of the vote in larger cities like Tehran, Esfahan, Tabriz, etc., Ahmedinejad enjoyed massive support from the provinces and small towns.[59]

Behind the smokescreen of redistribution, though, the Ahmedinejad agenda seems to have been essentially to give the *Sepah* and particularly the *Basijis* access to a larger share of the country's resources. Quite apart from appointing his fellow *Basijis* to most positions in the myriad public offices at all levels, Ahmedinejad orchestrated the privatisation policy in such a manner that they rank among the principal beneficiaries of the divestment of nationalised resources carried out since 2006.[60] Thus, privatisation, which was meant to mobilise capital for industrial development and in particular for reinvestment in Iran's sanction-ridden oil sector, was instead carried out in the opposite direction where the state actually lost capital assets.

There were increasing levels of discomfort even within the ranks of the traditional Conservatives, aligned to the *bazaar*. But, the gravity of the situation hit the Iranian establishment really hard after the global economic slowdown of 2008, which sharply pushed down global oil demand, and hence oil prices. This nevertheless did not reduce cost of Iran's imports of refined oil, forcing Ahmedinejad to rethink his opposition to fuel subsidies. In December 2010, fuel subsidies had to be cut by $20 billion, pushing ex-pump oil prices up by 400-900%.[61] The roll-back of subsidies pushed prices up all across the economy, hitting not only Ahmedinejad's core social constituencies hard, but also that of the Conservatives.

From this point on, the split between the traditional conservatives (i.e. the Osulgiran) and the neo-conservatives (Abadgaran) proved irretrievable. A consensus began to emerge among the traditional conservatives that for the economy to recover, sanctions (imposed on Iran by the international community on account of their suspicion about a covert nuclear military programme) had to be removed. This in turn required some understanding with the international community which Ahmedinejad could not be trusted with after years of brinkmanship on the issue. Hence Khamenei took charge, briefing the nuclear negotiators from that point on.

The turmoil of 2009 happened at a time when this divide and the distance between Khamenei and Ahmedinejad were obvious to the Iranians, and presumably the reformists fancied their chances that the traditional conservatives would not underwrite a second term for Ahmedinejad. While the Guardians and the Rahbar were not in favour of Ahmedinejad anymore, they were keen on retaining the political establishment that was at stake. Once Ahmedinejad's position was saved, though, the task of developing a larger political consensus was undertaken – both on the issue of nuclear programme, and on the need for larger economic restructuring. In a curious way, this went to vindicate the reformist agenda of both Rafsanjani and Khatami. Which is why after Rafsanjani's renewed attempt to run for the President's office in 2013 was foiled by the Guardians, both he and Khatami weighed in with their support for Hassan Rouhani. Whether this turns out to be a second wind for the Reform movement in Iran remains to be seen.

The Evolving Discourse of Popular Sovereignty: Ra'i Man Kujast?

Should one dissociate the discourse of politics from the politics itself? Does a discourse shape itself with time as politics moves on, or does politics revolve within the parameters laid down by the discourse? It is worth sticking one's neck out to argue that while political discourse always shapes itself within specific historical context, at each conjuncture it tends to be argued that politics *necessarily* revolves within the frames of a particular discourse – i.e. practitioners and theorists try to have the discourse set the limits within which politics must operate. A close observation of the political discourse of the Islamic Republic clearly shows that both the minimalist and the maximalist positions on popular sovereignty have developed within a larger matrix of events that are shaped not so much by cultural specificities (i.e. tenets of Shi'i Islam) as by political contingency.

In the Iranian political system that has evolved after the end of the Iraq War and the death of Khomeini, the contestation has been essentially over *how* is the sovereignty to be exercised by the people, ***not*** *whether* they are sovereign. Thus under the Constitution of the Islamic Republic, Khoemini was chosen the *Rahbar* **on account of** his recognition as such by the "majority of the people". The amendments made in the wake of Khoemeini's death in 1989 recognised that since Rahbars no longer commanded the spiritual and legal stature that Khomeini enjoyed, hence they would be chosen for their political sagacity by a body (the *Khobregan*) that was in their turn directly elected by the people, and could be even be removed by the body if he was found incapable of guidance to the Republic. Hence, arguably, the most powerful seat of unrepresentative authority in the Islamic Republic owes its legitimacy ultimately to the people, even if indirectly.

The minimalist discourse of popular sovereignty, as this essay has tried to argue, evolved primarily in the 1990s to thwart an attempt at liberalising the regime. Finding both the directly elected President and the *Majlis* the principal organisations of the proposed restructuring, the social groups that benefited directly and materially from the wartime revolutionary regime tried to preserve the existing apparatus by minimising the scope of exercise of popular sovereignty. Hence, in 1991, the Guardians announced its role to be *nezarat-e istesavi* (approval supervisory), which implied that all candidates to the *Majlis* had to be accepted by the Guardians – and the benchmark of such acceptance was not to be whether such candidates could or did promote the (short-term) interests of the people, rather whether they upheld Islam and the Islamic order (which represented their long-term interests). Khamenei, the other nodal point of unrepresentative authority in the Islamic Republic, underwrote this position soon after saying:

> If someone speaks and writes in opposition to the views of the *faqih*, he is opposed to the principle of *vilayat-e faqih*, and therefore the Islamic order itself. ... As a rule... it is better if you do not select these people. If there is no proof or evidence against them [being opposed to the *vilayat-e faqih*}, you can act based on your knowledge.[62]

When attempts were made to resist this measure, the language was distinctively that of a more maximalist reading of the same concept – as was done by Musavi-Khoeiniha who argued that "[t]he regime belongs to the people and they are its own guardians."[63] A far more powerful challenge to the minimalist reading came from Khatami, whose views were premised upon the need for *tahamol* (toleration) as a *sine qua non* for strengthening civil society (*jame'h-ye madani*) and rule of law (*hokumat-e qanun*) in the Islamic Republic. Careful enough not to challenge the foundational principle of the Islamic Republic, the *Vilayat-e Faqih*, Khatami claimed his agenda of institutionalisation of rule of law in Iran and creation of a democratic order was the inherent purpose behind Ruhollah Khomeini's doctrine of rule by the Jurist. Arguing that the systematic decline in voter turn-out undermined the very legitimacy of the Islamic regime, Khatami subtly challenged the pre-dominant conservative position that the Islamic Republic derived its legitimacy primarily from Islam and not the people. Khatami argued that the Islamic Revolution of 1979 was motivated by the need to establish a democratic society, which was the defining feature of the Islamic order that Imam Khomeini had meant to institute.[64] Khatami believed the vicious political culture that had emerged in the Islamic regime, confusing dissent with enmity, undermined the very basis of that intention. He championed instead the notion of *chandarzeshi* (pluralism), which implied equal legitimacy of all the different approaches to the Islamic order, and identified the need for *tahamol* to accommodate such divergent approaches.

Once Ahmedinejad came to power, given the vicious crackdown on the social and cultural freedoms, this expansive understanding of popular sovereignty and the principle of *tahamol* was in jeopardy. The intolerance that characterised the response of the Conservative establishment generated a deep sense of alienation among the upwardly mobile urban middle class, who had blossomed in the ambience of social and cultural freedom during the Khatami years. Thus, the popular demonstrations of 2009-10 on the streets of urban Iran bearing banners asking “Ra’i man kujast” (Where is my vote) were not so much an assertion of popular sovereignty against a regime that denies it (as was the case in the Arab world), rather an expression of alienation from regime that has become unresponsive to the concerns of the people. Such a reading of the turmoil appears to be borne out by the outcome of the presidential election of 2013, which has seen a candidate with a proven reformist credential emerge with a larger tally of seats than all the conservative candidates put together – not unlike a safety valve letting off steam.

Conclusion

In Iran, as much as in many other places in the developing world, the principle of popular sovereignty is a contested domain. Unlike in many other places in the Middle East, the Iranians are ahead of most of their neighbours in that political legitimacy in the Islamic Republic is recognised as emanating from the people. The battle however is ongoing in terms of the manner in which the people exercise their sovereignty. As elsewhere in the Middle East, the weaker the state becomes, the prospects of democracy (and therewith direct exercise of sovereign power by the direct representatives of the people) improve – as was quite evident from the wave that carried first Khatami to power, and now appears to have put Rouhani at the helm. Indeed, the fortunes of political reform in the Islamic Republic improve mostly whenever the regime is under duress. However, the space the body-politic allows for the principle of popular sovereignty, and the establishment's ability to reform itself enables it to save the Islamic Republic from the still greater danger of systemic collapse.

Notes

1. *Ettela'at*, June 15th 2009.
2. "Hatred, Chaos and Savage Beatings in Tehran" CNN International, 15th June 2009, http://edition.cnn.com/2009/WORLD/meast/06/14/iran.eyewitness/index.html [accessed on 16th June 2009]
3. "Tehran tense as Iran's Supreme Leader endorses vote outcome", CNN International, 15th June 2009, http://edition.cnn.com/2009/WORLD/meast/06/14/iran.election/ [accessed on 16th June 2009]
4. Andrew Lavalle, "Web users in Iran reach for proxies overseas", *Digits,* 15th June 2009, [accessed on 22nd March 2012], http://blogs.wsj.com/digits/2009/06/15/web-users-in-iran-reach-overseas-for-proxies/
5. See, for instance Farhang Jahanpour, "Iran's stolen elections and what comes next", *Open Democracy* 18th June 2009, http://www.opendemocracy.net/article/iran-s-stolen-election-and-what-comes-next [accessed on 25th June 2009]; Ahmad Salamatian, "Iran's stolen election", *Frontline,* 7 July 2009, http://www.pbs.org/wgbh/pages/frontline/tehranbureau/2009/07/irans-stolen-election.html [accessed on 31st July 2009]; Juan Cole, "Stealing the Iranian Election," *Informed Comment*, 13th June, 2009, http://www.juancole.com/2009/06/stealing-iranian-election.html [accessed on 31st July 2009]; Stephen Zune, "Iran's stolen elections have sparked an uprising – what should the US do?" *the World Post,* 15th June 2009, http://www.huffingtonpost.com/stephen-zunes/irans-stolen-election-has_b_215472.html [accessed on 30th June 2009].
6. For one of the earliest academic studies casting doubt on the verdict , see Ali Ansari (ed.), *Preliminary Analysis of the Voting Figures in Iran's 2009 Presidential Election*, MENAP PP 2009/01, http://www.chathamhouse.org/sites/default/files/public/Research/Middle%20East/iranelection0609.pdf [accessed on 1st March 2013].

7. Farhang Jahanpour, "Iran's stolen elections and what comes next", *Open Democracy* 18th June 2009, http://www.opendemocracy.net/article/iran-s-stolen-election-and-what-comes-next [accessed on 25th June 2009]
8. *Keyhan,* 13th June 2009.
9. See Reza Esfandiari, Yousef Bozorgmehr, "A rejoinder to the Chatham House Report on Iran's 2009 presidential election offering a new analysis on the results ", http://www.iranaffairs.com/files/iranian-election.pdf [accessed on 13th March 2013].
10. Ahmad Salamatian, "Iran's stolen election", *Frontline,* 7th July 2009, http://www.pbs.org/wgbh/pages/frontline/tehranbureau/2009/07/irans-stolen-election.html [accessed on 31st July 2009]; Tony Karon, "Khamenei: the Power Behind the President," *Time*, 15th June 2009, http://content.time.com/time/world/article/0,8599,1904589,00.html
11. Mousavi was the Prime Minister of Iran during the period when Khamenei was the President, at a time when the Prime Minister was the chief executive office, while the President was merely a figurehead Head of State.
12. Robert Worth, "Ahmedinejad submits a cabinet of acolytes", *New York Times*, 19th August 2009, http://www.nytimes.com/2009/08/20/world/middleeast/20iran.html?_r=0
13. *Ettela'at*, 16th June 2009.
14. *Ettela'at*, 17th June 2009.
15. Chris Emery, "Khamenei's Supreme Dilemma", 17th June 2009 , *the Guardian.com* http://www.theguardian.com/commentisfree/2009/jun/17/khameini-iran-ahmadinejad-mousavi [accessed on 20th March 2013).
16. *Ettela'at*, 18th June 2009.
17. *Jomhuri Islami*, 18th June 2009.
18. *Ettela'at*, 19th June, 2009.
19. www.theguardian.com/world/2009/jun/19/iran-elections-ayatollah-ali-khamenei
20. "Iran: Mir Hossein Mousavi and Mehdi Karroubi arrested", 28th February 2011, http://www.bbc.co.uk/news/world-middle-east-12599837
21. Mir Hossein-Mousavi was the Prime Minister of Iran (1981-89). Mehdi Karroubi held the chairmanship of the *Majlis* during 1989-92 and 2000-04. Additionally, Karroubi is a nominated member of the Expediency Council.
22. For a critical account of the Pahlavi era in Iran, see Ervand Abrahamian, *Iran Between Two Revolutions*, (Princeton, NJ: Princeton University Press, 1982), Homa Katouzian, *The Political Economy of Modern Iran: Despotism and Pseudo-Modernism 1926-79*, (London and New York: Macmillan and New York University Press, 1981).
23. For a very comprehensive account and analysis of the Iranian political system under the Islamic Republic, see Asghar Schirazi, *The Constitution of Iran: Politics and*

State in the Islamic Republic, [translated by John O'Hara], (London: I.B. Tauris, 1997),

24. The President is responsible for the national budget, planning, law and order, and foreign relations of the Republic. He is also responsible for the process of recruitment, appointment and removal of public servants in all government organs.
25. Authorised to delineate the general policies of the Islamic Republic and supervise its proper functioning, the *Rahbar* is the supreme commander of the armed forces in the Islamic Republic, and is accordingly authorised to declare war, peace and mobilisation of armed forces. He is also authorised to appoint a large number of constitutional functionaries – such as the commanders of armed forces, head of the judiciary, the *fuqaha* (Islamic jurists) on the Guardians Council – who are accountable only to the *Rahbar.*
26. It also functions as an advisory body for the *Rahbar*. Asghar Schirazi, *The Constitution of Iran: Politics and State in the Islamic Republic*, [translated by John O'Hara], (London: I.B. Tauris, 1997), p. 64.
27. All legislative measures passed by the *Majlis* have to be reviewed by the Guardians to ensure the compatibility of such measures with both Islam and the Constitution of the Islamic Republic, and they are further vested with the responsibility of interpretation of the Constitution. Still more significantly, the Guardians claim the authority to screen the candidates for the Presidency, the *Majlis*, the *Khobregan* and the various other elective offices at national and regional levels, and (arguably) to eliminate candidates with either doubtful Islamic credentials or doubtful loyalty towards the Islamic Republic.
28. Art. 56 of the Iranian constitution.
29. Art. 56 of the Iranian constitution.
30. The term 'hierocracy' is a neologism coined by Sayyid Amir Arjomand, referring specifically to the Shi'i religious institutional apparatus in Iran. See, Arjomand, *The Shadow of God and the Hidden Imam: Religion, Political Order and Societal Change in Shi 'ite Iran Beginning to 1890*, (Chicago: Chicago University Press, 1984).
31. The Islamic Republic is replete with such examples. Khomeini, the first *Rahbar*, tended to avoid interfering as much as possible in the day-to-day task of administration, but when the socially conservative and free trading forces in the *Majlis* resisted the regulated economic order erected by the left-leaning Prime Minister Mir Hossein-Mousavi in the mid-80s during the Iraq War, the *Rahbar* felt compelled to weigh in on the side of Mousavi. At that stage, the social conservatives were keen to establish that the *Rahbar* was meant to guide, not govern; that the *Majlis* is the only organ authorised to frame the directions for policy, and the executive was to merely implement it. At that stage, the leftist elements in the revolutionary order favoured Khomeini's intervention because it broke the deadlock in their favour.

After the death of Khomeini, once the socially conservative Khamenei was elevated to the position of the *Rahbar*, the conservatives began favour the *Rahbar's* right to intervene, because such intervention began to be in favour of the conservative-dominated *Majlis*. Similarly, the left-wingers who had once basked in the support of the *Rahbar* and happily accepted his intervention as legitimate, have since the end of the war found similar intervention as infringement of popular sovereignty. See Mehdi Moslem, *Factional Politics in Post-Khomeini Iran*. (New York: Syracuse University Press, 2002); Hossein S. Seifzadeh, 'The Landscape of Factional Politics and its Future in Iran', *Middle East Journal*, vol. 57, no. 1, Winter 2003, pp. 57-75.

32. The label Conservatives would cover distinct but analogous groups from different periods after 1979, almost all of whom favour a regulated social and cultural space with little government control over the economy. In the 1980s, this denoted the right-wing members of the Hizb-e Jomhuri-ye Islami (Islamic Republic Party), with which the *bazaar* was closely associated. From the late 1980s, after the IRP was dissolved, the *Jame'h-e Rouhaniyun-e Mobarez* (Society of Combatant Clergy) constituted the bedrock of the Conservatives, and gradually began to work in tandem with the party of the lay politicians known as the *Jamiyat-e Motalefeh-ye Islami* (Allied Islamic Society, or Motalefeh for short, led by people like Mohsen Rafiqdust and the Larijani brothers), which has dominated the conservative block from the Khatami years. By 2008, the JRM-Motalefeh axis began to label itself as *A'etelaf-e Firagir-e Osulgirian* or the Osulgirian (Principalists) for short. The agenda that Mahmoud Ahmedinejad came to represent combined social conservatism of the traditional conservatives with a redistributive economic agenda – they are known as the *A'etelaf-e Abadagaran-e Iran-e Islami* (Alliance of Builders of Islamic Iran), or the Abadgaran for short.

33. The Reformist would connote, as for the Conservatives, different but analogous formations at different points of time. Reformists tended to be united by their emphasis on freedom in the social and cultural arena. Their economic agenda tended to be divided between votaries of a regulated economy (viz. Hossein Mousavi) in the 1980s and free marketeers (Rafsanjani), but in the 1990s they have veered increasingly towards lesser state control of the economy. Thus in the early 1980s, they would be found in the left wing of the HII/IRP; by late-1980s they would come to be found in the Majme'h-ye Rouhaniyun-e Mobarez (Association of Combatant Clergymen). During the Rafsanjani era, the right-of-centre outfit of the *Hizb-e Kargozaran-e Sazandagi* (Party of the Executives of the Reconstruction) came to combine with them to make up the Reformist movement known as the *Dovvom-e Khordad*.

34. Sohrab Behdad, 'From Populism to Liberalism: the Iranian Predicament', in Parvin Alizadeh, *The Economy of Iran: Dilemmas of an Islamic State*, (London and New York: I.B. Tauris, 2000), p. 113.

35. *Kayhan Havaii,* 24th August 1991.
36. Bijan Khajehpour, 'Iran's Economy: Twenty Years after the Islamic Revolution', in Anourshivan Ehteshami, *After Khomeini: the Iranian Second Republic*, (London: Routledge, 1995), p. 97.
37. For a very comprehensive treatment of Iran's economic liberalisation under Rafsanjani, see Sohrab Behdad, 'From Populism to Liberalism', pp. 115-31.
38. The Foundations were initially economic foundations and organisations owned by either the Shah's family or his cronies, which were nationalised with a redistributive purpose. This was followed by nationalisation of the assets of the 51 largest industrialists in the early months of the revolution. For a description of the major industrial families under the Shah and the process of nationalisation, see Ehteshami, *After Khomeini*, pp. 83-8.
39. In order to maintain necessary levels of production, the government transferred management of industries to young inexperienced revolutionaries while nearly a million professionals fled the country under the organisational framework of Foundations.. Suzanne Maloney, 'Agents or Obstacles: Parastatal Foundations and Challenges for Iranian Development', in Alizadeh, *The Economy of Iran*, p. 154.
40. For a brief treatment of the role played by the *Sepah* and the *Basij*, see Frederic Wehrey, Jerrold D. Green, Brian Nichiporuk, Alireza Nader, Lydia Hansell, Rasool Nafisi, S. R. Bohandy, *The Rise of the Pasdaran*: *Assessing the Domestic Roles of the Islamic Revolutionary Guards Corps*, (Arlington VA, RAND Corporation, 2009)
41. Moslem, *Factional Politics,* p. 171.
42. *Salaam*, 24th November, 1992.
43. During the 1980s, the *Basij* forces had worked in tandem with the regime to physically crush all domestic opposition. Frequently such activities took the form of enforcing Islamic virtues and punishing immoral or lax behaviour on part of the people, and were constitutionally underwritten by the injunction to engage in *amr beh al-ma'ruf wa nahy an'l munkar* (lit. Enjoin what is known [to be Good] and Forbidding the Evil). Determined to create a more open and free society, Rafsanjani was particularly wary of *Basij* tactics of physical assault and summary punishment. His support for the policies of Khatami, thus, was directly in opposition to modus operandi of the *Basij*.
44. Previously, to be elected to the Experts, eligible candidates needed to be fully acquainted with the basis of *ijtihad* (independent legal reasoning) and educated at prominent *howzeh* (seminaries) 'to the degree of being able to discern competency for the *marja'iyat* and *Rahbariyat*.' The eligibility of candidates was discerned by attestation of three well-known teachers of *howzeh*, or by general recognition of the candidates as a *mujtahid* (capable of independent legal reasoning) in religious circles, or attestation from the *Rahbar* himself. After the changes brought in 1990,

it was sufficient for the candidates to be eligible to infer on issues of *fiqh* (Islamic jurisprudence), which would be subject to a competency test evaluated by the Guardians. Secondly attestation by prominent teachers of the *howzeh* was no longer acceptable; either the leader or the *fuqaha* among the Guardians had to testify to a candidate's eligibility. See, Moslem, *Factional Politics*, pp. 156-57.

45. The *Basij* had begun to lose its relevance after the end of the Iraq war, and found it reasonably difficult to reinvent itself. Unlike the main core of the *Sepah*, which had gained access to industrial and other economic enterprises, the *Basij* did not quite benefit materially from the period of economic reconstruction that characterised the Rafsanjani era. Thus the predominantly lower-middle class elements of the *Basij* found in the November 1992 laws a vindication of its continued existence. The Basij became particularly active in the two arena were that ambience of cultural freedom had become most conspicuous – the municipal parks and the universities – and which provided the real catchments of leftist politics. With its vigilante activities given constitutional authorisation and endorsed by the conservative forces and the *Rahbar* himself, the *Basiji*s in general and the *Setad* became active in endorsing a strict morality code in public place, especially in the municipal parks and the universities. The *Basiji*s targeting of the universities being aimed specifically at breaking up leftist student unions under the cover of enforcement of Islamic morality (viz. segregation of the sexes in public place, proper dress code, etc), the influential student organisation *Daftar-e Tahkim-e Vahdat* (Office of Strengthening of Unity) fought out a vicious turf war in the universities.
46. *Salaam*, May 28th 1997.
47. Moslem, *Factional Politics,* p. 255.
48. *Salaam*, 31st October 1997.
49. *Resalat*, 25th August 1997.
50. Ibid. p. 11.
51. Despite the usual debarring of left-wing and centrist candidates by the Guardians, in the sixth *Majlis*, the reformist *Dovvom-e Khordad* coalition secured 65% of the votes, and 189 of the 270 *Majlis* seats; the conservatives got 19% of the votes and 54 seats with 42 going to the independents.
52. Bijan Khajehpour, 'Iran's Economy,' p. 114.
53. For a brief but comprehensive treatment of the Third Plan, see Khajehpour, 'Iran's Economy', pp. 114-119. Khatami's attack on the Foundations won the most (probably the only) significant victory in July 1999, when Mohsen Rafiqdust, the influential director of the wealthiest *bonyad*, the *Bonyad-e Mostazafin*, had to be replaced after being continuously shielded by Khamenei throughout the Rafsanjani era. His replacement, former minister of defence Muhammad Foruzandeh, had to pledge cooperation with the government. See Suzanne Maloney, 'Agents or Obstacles?', p. 167.

54. "Oil Price History and Analysis", http://www.wtrg.com/prices.htm [accessed 20th March, 2013]
55. In 2001, these *bonyads* operated hundreds of companies, receive more than half of the state's annual expenditures in terms of economic activities, and account for up to 40% of the country's economy. See, Maloney, "agents or Obstacles".
56. Ali Rezaei, 'Last Effort of Iran's Reformists', *Middle East Report*, no. 226, Spring 2003, p. 41.
57. In 2005, when the prices began to rise sharply, Iran's oil export revenue stood at $46.6 billion, double the high point of the Khatami presidency of $23.7 billion in 2003. As oil prices jumped from $55 per barrel to $147, Iran's oil export stood at $70 billion – more than two and a half times the average for the Khatami period. http://www.payvand.com/news/09/feb/1034.html [accessed on 1st May, 2009]
58. Under a new law regarding 'privatisation' introduced by Ahmedinejad, nearly 2,000 nationalised entities valued at anything between $100 and 140 billion were privatised. Almost 40% of the shares so divested were earmarked as "justice shares" for sale among low income households at heavily discounted prices. The value of such resources made over to 4.6 million people has been put at $2.7 billion. See Nader Habibi, "The Economic Legacy of Mahmoud Ahmedinejad", *Middle East Brief, Crown Centre for Middle East Studies*, p. 3. http://www.brandeis.edu/crown/publications/meb/MEB74.pdf [accessed on 31st January 2014]
59. Esfandiari and Bozorgmehr, "A rejoinder to the Chatham House Report" pp. 7-10.
60. Eligibility for the "justice shares" was, primarily, participation in the Iraq War, which allowed both the Sepah and the Basij veterans to get these. Additionally, 40% of these shares were released in the stock market, but having barely any takers who were willing to invest in enterprises in which they could not have controlling stake, even these shares were purchased by Foundations dominated by the Sepah and the Basij. Habibi, "Economic Legacy" p. 3.
61. Kayhan, 20th December 2010.
62. *Salaam,* 24th February 1992.
63. *Salaam,* 10th March 1992.
64. *Salaam*, 28th November 1997.